Valentio
Di' Buondelmonte

Valentio Di' Buondelmonte

A Tragedy in Five Acts

HAIG KHATCHADOURIAN

With a Foreword by Roy Arthur Swanson

RESOURCE *Publications* · Eugene, Oregon

VALENTIO DI' BUONDELMONTE
A Tragedy in Five Acts

Copyright © 2014 Haig Khatchadourian. All rights reserved. Except for brief quotations in critical publications or reviews, no part of this book may be reproduced in any manner without prior written permission from the publisher. Write: Permissions, Wipf and Stock Publishers, 199 W. 8th Ave., Suite 3, Eugene, OR 97401.

Resource Publications
An Imprint of Wipf and Stock Publishers
199 W. 8th Ave., Suite 3
Eugene, OR 97401

www.wipfandstock.com

ISBN 13: 978-1-62564-212-7

Manufactured in the U.S.A.

To Arpiné

I come, Great Friend, fearful yet rich in hope,
To place upon the Altar of thy heart
This humble wreathe of daisies wild, gathered
From the untrodden fields of my lone soul,
Woven by unskilled fingers rude, albeit
Fain would I have them be of roses proud.
....
O if the random notes of my wild song,
Swept on my heart's frail strings but newly strung,
Strike discords harsh upon they dainty ear,
I know thou wilt not scorn my faltering art,
Since they will be to thee Symbol and Sign
Of my tongue-less (save Silence) esteem for thee:
For when the notes are done and dead, Silence
And silent looks become articulate.

Contents

Foreword

ix

Introduction

xv

Dramatis Personae

xix

Part One
Original Version: A Five-Act blank verse Tragedy, in Elizabethan English

1

Part Two
A New Version of the Tragedy in free verse, in modern English

67

Foreword

In *Valentio Di' Buondelmonte* Professor Haig Khatchadourian gives today's readers a sample of Elizabethan English and an example of a Renaissance tragedy; in doing so, he has produced an exemplar of illustration.

The words "sample," "example," and "exemplar" are all derived from the Latin *exemplum*, but they intimate a qualitative progression that advances beyond the "copy / original" distinction of *exemplum / exemplaris*. Generally, a sample is a partial representation, an example is a full or summary representation, and an exemplar is a prime meritorious representation. Aristotle, in his Poetics, provides samples (incidents in) and examples (summaries) of bad and good works of tragedy. For him, the exemplar of tragedy is Sophocles's *Oedipus Tyrannos*, representing the sixfold acme of *mythos* (plot), *ethos* (character), *dianoia* (thought), *lexis* (diction), *melopoeia* (musical sonance), and *opsis* (visual attraction). Shakespeare's *Hamlet* meets much of Aristotle's complex criterion and may be considered an (if not *the*) exemplar of Elizabethan tragedy; but its elements of revenge, emotional conflict, Stoicism, and moralism betray its greater debt to Senecan rather than to Sophoclean tragedy. In his appropriation of Elizabethan diction and revenge-preoccupation, Professor Khatchadourian has produced a sampling of emotional excess (as opposed to Attic restraint), an example of Elizabethan *mythos* (plot that is oriented more from emotional vagaries than from *peripeteia* [reversal of expectations and circumstances] and *anagnorisis* [belated discovery], although inclusive of Attic *pathos* [suffering]), and an exemplar of *mimesis* (melding Attic and Senecan imitations of *praxis* [action] in a literary scholar's imitation of Elizabethan *lexis* and *pathos*. His subsequent translation of *Valentio Di'Buondelmonte* into modern English offers readers a means of

Foreword

measuring, in the context of *melopoeia* (including, in both versions: rhetorical figuration, such as alliteration and metaphor, and continuity in iambic pentameter), a variation of emotionalism between Elizabethan and current English.

Here is a slight but significant sample of his variation:

[Elizabethan] She is /A virgin rose but newly blown from the bud.
[Modern] She's a virgin rose newly blown from the bud. . . .

The unilinear modern statement excludes ambiguity: "She's a virgin rose" precludes a reading of "rose" as a verb. The Elizabethan statement invites such a reading: "She is," set off from the following line and uncontracted, may be read as "She exists" and "A virgin rose [*verb*]"; it also retains the metaphor, "She is a rose . . . newly blown." Moreover, "but" serves both as "only" or "just" and as an adversative. As a poet, Professor Khatchadourian knows that ambiguity adds applicable connotation to basic denotation and compounds the significance of a statement. As a philosopher, he appreciates the extended mental journeys that functional ambiguity initiates: movement in two different but complementary directions at the same time. Both Ludwig Wittgenstein and Martin Heidegger observe this variability as Language's spiritual game. In the context of "tragedy," then, the poet-philosopher shows us how Elizabethan English can enhance our experience of language. This answers the question, "Why write an Elizabethan tragedy today?" and establishes the nature of the composition.

A well-established basis for tragic drama is what Aristotle calls plots centering on some houses (μύθους . . . περ λίγας οκίας). By "houses" we may understand families or political entities—or economic classes, and, ultimately, ways of life. Aristotle mentions the houses (or families, or partisans) of Alcmaeon, Oedipus, Orestes, Meleager, Thyestes, and Telephus. Common among such plots of houses in conflict is that of a young man romantically attached to a young woman whose family stands in opposition to his own. For example, Alcmaeon, married to Phegeus's daughter Alphesiboea, deserts his wife to consort with Achelous's daughter Callirrhoë, for whom he strives to recover the magical necklace (of Harmonia) that he had given to Alphesiboea and is therein killed by Phegeus's

Foreword

sons. The love of Shakespeare's Romeo and Juliet brings the houses of Montague and Capulet to similarly motivated bloodshed. Professor Khatchadourian explains that *Valentio Di' Buondelmonte* is "inspired by Shakespeare's tragedies, which follow" classical Greek tragic themes. Valentio agrees to marry Beatrice of the Ameidei family as a means of resolving the hostility between that family and his. But his first sight of Livia di' Donati compels him to break his engagement to Beatrice and devote his life and love to Livia, who fully requites his devotion. Beatrice, in her turn, loves and elopes with Uberto, a friend of Valentio. The familial feud is explosively exacerbated. Valentio is assassinated for his desertion of Beatrice. Uberto is killed in his attempt to avenge Valentio. Beatrice, like Shakespeare's Juliet, commits suicide in her grief over the death of her beloved. Livia, bereft of Valentio, takes Beatrice's knife and contemplates suicide, uttering a soliloquy reminiscent of Hamlet's "To be or not to be"; then, hearing the assassins calling for death to the Donati and Buondelmonti and specifically to her mother, who had engineered the attachment of herself and Valentio, Livia exits to end the drama.

Professor Khatchadourian's drama, with its Shakespearean echoes, carries forth the *lexis* and *melopoeia* of Elizabethan tragedy. By way of example, a citizen says, "This sound is new to my ears"; a second citizen says, "Lend them to me, then . . ."; and we are reminded of Antony's speech to the citizens in *Julius Caesar*. Uberto's "For lo! The betraying streaks / Of day from yonder Orient gates of Heaven / Do rend the velvet folds of friendly night" is consonant with Horatio's "But, look, the morn in russet mantle clad, / Walks o'er the dew of yon high eastward hill" (*Hamlet* I.1.166–7). The fury of Elizabethan tragedy reflects humankind's incompatibility with its own species and the failure of love as a force to neutralize or contain violence. In *Valentio*, Uberto points to a statue of Mars as "this grim idol / Of fire and fury"; and "idol" is understood both as "false god" and "object of adoration," just as the bloodshed of Elizabethan tragedy is both harrowing and entertaining.

Shakespeare's *Macbeth* (V.5.26–8) contains the titular speaker's lament that life is "a tale / Told by an idiot, full of sound and fury, /Signifying nothing." Elizabethan tragedy, filled with sound and fury, signifies that idiocy is a form of self-centered orientation alien to altruism (Greek idios means "one's own self"; Latin *alter* means "other"). To this effect, Beatrice's long pre-suicidal lament, brilliantly wrought in *Valentio*, is inescapably Elizabethan, including the following: ". . . Love, Lord of the Soul, before / Whose sovereignty Friendship should bend the knee / Of homage meek, hath risen in rash rebellion, / His throne usurping, claiming obedience low / Of him who knows how to receive, but not / To give. . . ." Idiocy, self-induced blindness to the Other, is, in fact, the gene of obsession.

Virginia Woolf, to whom this idiocy is manifest in her phrase (from *A Room of One's Own*) "Milton's bogey," catches this note of human antithesis in *Orlando*. The comic novel opens with young Orlando entertaining himself by "slicing at the head of a [slain] Moor which hung from the rafters." The cultural setting of the first part of the novel is Elizabethan England, in which Shakespeare's plays (especially *Othello*) are very popular. Orlando, engaged to marry Lady Margaret, deserts her and falls wholly in love with Marousha ("Sasha"), a Russian princess, in much the same way that Valentio falls in love with Livia. "Sasha" requites his love but arbitrarily deserts him. The force of Orlando's love-at-first-sight is a kind of violence; it is, indeed, quite similar to Valentio's obsessive love of Livia at first sight and to his consequent desertion of Beatrice. Obsession is a violent emotion, a willful blocking of one's vision from all but the immediate object of one's desire; and it is akin to hostility. Woolf seems to see a resolution of love and war only in fantasy, the pursuit of which can lead to the essence of reality in the exercise of the imagination. For her, Elizabethan tragedy records a failure of imagination, a failure from which, significantly, we can learn.

Obsession in Elizabethan tragedy ranges from culturally conflicted emotions (the wars of houses) to individually self-centered emotions, including those "*che sono vili*" ("that are villainous"), as Professor Khatchadourian observes in *Il tragico e l'irrazionale* [*Rivista di Estetica*, XII.1, Jan.–Apr. 1967, p. 73], like the ambition of Macbeth and Lady Macbeth. Obsession is never benign; and in Elizabethan tragedy love is measured on the scales of obsession.

Foreword

It is important to learn that to be obsessed is to be possessed by the notion of what one wants to possess. The lover, requited or unrequited in desire, wants to possess the wherewithal to secure her or his beloved. Star-crossed lovers want to possess the freedom to consummate their love. Families want to possess their integrity securely by keeping their integers within the strictly defined familial unit. Lovers and families provide the context for the sound and fury of Elizabethan tragedy. With individuals, it is love (or what is taken to be love: a receipt of satisfaction more than a giving of it). With families, it is feuds. With nations, it is wars. From the star-crossed lovers (Valentio and Livia; Uberto and Beatrice) in Professor Khatchadourian's tragedy we proceed to the feud between the Ameidei and the Buondelmonti. And then, as we learn from his introduction, there would be the Guelf and Ghibelline factions, "and long after the original cause of enmity had ceased, they continued to steep all Italy in blood."

As Virginia Woolf and Haig Khatchadourian intimate effectively, the trail from love to war is blazed by obsession. Love is, not a unilateral donation of the self to the other, but an uncompromising need to be satisfied by possession of the other. That Aphrodite and Ares should embrace and produce Harmonia is a product of the imagination. According to Woolf, the essence of reality is to be found in the imagination. Khatchadourian thus fires his imagination by shaping historical shadows into Elizabethan tragic poetry. He restates and adumbrates an answer to the question that Woolf has promulgated in *Orlando*. Woolf has playfully parodied Elizabethan culture and imaginatively equated the sexes by changing her male Orlando into a female Orlando in mid-story. Khatchadourian evokes Elizabethan culture by recapturing its music and force and tracing the genesis of its dramatic creativity to ancient Greece. Both enable us inspiritedly to exercise the imagination in coping with the phenomenon of idiocy. That, one may conclude, is in accordance with what is exemplary.

Roy Arthur Swanson
Emeritus Professor of Classics and Comparative Literature
The University of Wisconsin-Milwaukee

Introduction

The original play, consisting of Part One of this book, inspired by Shakespeare's tragedies, was written in blank verse in Elizabethan English, many decades ago, during the author's Junior Year at the American University of Beirut, Lebanon. It follows, like Shakespeare's tragedies, the Classical Greek Tragedies in its thematic and structural elements, including *ignorance* and *discovery*, the *climax* and the *denouement*, as well as the tragic character's Achilles' heel—*error of judgment* (*hamartia*)—formalized by Aristotle in the *Poetics*, In 2012 a new version, in free verse, in modern English, was added for the benefit of readers unfamiliar with Elizabethan English.

The source of the Tragedy consists in a series of historical events in 1215 Florence that resulted in protracted internecine conflict involving a number of leading families. The following passages, culled from a long-lost history book, provided the works' inspiration.

"In Florence, the city that prided itself on being founded under the protection and ascendant of Mars, and therefore doomed by fate to everlasting troubles. Hence Roccuzzo de Mozzi is made by Dante to say:

> Io fui della citta, che nel Batista
> Cangio iL primo Padrone, onde ei per questo
> Sempre con L'arte sua la fara trista.

In the year 1215, Messer Mazzingo Tegrini invited many Florentines of high rank to dine at his villa near Campi about six miles from the capital; while at able the family jester snatched a trencher of meat from Messer Uberto degli Infangati who, nettled at this impertinence, expressed his displeasure in terms so offensive that Messer Oddo Arrighi as sharply and unceremoniously rebuked him; upon this Uberto gave him the lie and Oddo in return dashed a trencher of meat in his face.

Everything was immediately in confusion; weapons were soon out, and while the guests started up in disorder young Buondelmonte de'Buondelmonti, the friend and companion to Uberto, severely wounded Oddo Arrighi.

The party then separated and Oddo called a meeting of his friends to consider the offence; amongst them were the counts Gangalandi, the Ubverti, Amedidei, etc. who unanimously decided that the quarrel shoud be quietly settled by a marriage between Buondelmonte and Oddo's niece, the daughter of Messer Lambertuccio di Capo di Ponte, of the Ameidei family. This proposition appears to have been unhesitatingly accepted by the offender's family as a day was immediately nominated for the ceremony of plighting his troth to the destined bride.

During the interim, Madonna Aldruda Donati, sent privately for Buondelmonte and thus addressed him: "Unworthy knight! What! Hast thou accepted a wife through fear of the Fifanti and Uberti? Leave her that thou hast taken, choose this damsel in her place and be henceforth a brave and honoured gentleman." In so saying she threw open the chamber door, and exposed her daughter to his view; the unexpected apparition of so much beauty, as it were soliciting his love, had its usual consequence; Buondelmonte's better reason was overcome, yet he had resolution to answer, "Alas! it is now too late!" "No," replied Aldruda; "thou canst even yet have her; dare but to take the step and let the consequences rest on my head." "I do dare," returned the fascinated youth, and stepping forward again plighted a faith no longer his to give.

Early on the 10th of February, the very day appointed for his original nuptials, Buondelmonte passed by the Porta Santa Maria amidst all the kinsfolk of his first betrothed, who had assembled near the dwellings of the Ameidei to assist at the expected marriage, yet not without certain misgivings of his faithlessness. With a haughty demeanour he rode forward through them all, bearing the marriage ring to the lady of his choice and leaving her of the

Introduction

Ameidei with the shame of an aggravated insult by choosing the same moment for the violation of one contract and the consummation of a second; for in those days, and for centuries after, the old Roman custom of presenting a ring long before the marriage ceremony took place was still in use.

Such insults were then impatiently borne; Oddo assembled his kindred in the no-longer existing church of Santa Maria sopra Porta to settle the mode of resenting this affront, and the moody aspect of each individual marked the character of the meeting and all the vindictive feeling of an injured family. There were, however, some of a more temperate spirit that suggested personal chastisement of at most the gashing of Buondelmonte's face as the most reasonable and effectual retribution. The assembly paused, but Mosca de Lamberti starting suddenly forward exclaimed, "Beat or wound him as ye list but first prepare your own graves, for wounds bring equal consequences with death." "No. Mete him out his deserts and let him pay the penalty; but no delay. Up and be doing."

"This turned the scale and Buondelmonte was doomed. But according to the manners of that age, not in the field, which would have been hazardous, but by the sure though inglorious means of noonday murder; wherefore, at the very place where the insult was offered, beneath the battlements of the Ameidei, nay under the casement of the deserted maiden, and in his way to a happy expecting bride, vengeance was prepared by these fierce barons for the perjury.

On Easter morning, 1215, the murderers concealed themselves within the courts and towers of the Ameidei, which the young and heedless bridegroom was sure to pass, and he was soon after seen at a distance carelessly riding alone across the Ponte Vecchio on a milk-white palfrey, attired in a vest of fine woollen cloth, a white mantle thrown across his shoulders and the wedding garland on his head. The bridge was passed in thoughtless gaiety, but scarcely had he reached the time-worn image of the Roman Mars, the last relic of heathen worship then extant, when the mace of Schiatti degli Uberto felled him to the ground, and at the base of this grim idol the daggers of Oddo and his furious kinsmen finished the savage deed; they met him gay and adorned for the alter, and left him with the

Introduction

bridal wreath still dangling from his brow a bloody and ill-omened sacrifice. The tidings of this murder spread rapidly, and disordered the whole community of Florence; the people became more and more excited, because both law and custom had awarded due penalties for faithless men, and death was an unheard-of punishment. Buondelmonte's corpse was placed on a bier, with its head resting in the lap of his affianced bride, the beautiful Donati, who hung like a lily over the pallid features of her husband; and thus united were they borne through the streets of Florence. It was the gloomy dawning of a tempestuous day, for in that bloody moment was unchained the demon of Florentine discord; the names of Guelf and Ghibelline were then for the first time assumed by noble and commoner as the cry of faction; and long after the original cause of enmity had ceased, they continued to steep all Italy in blood."

Dramatis Personae

DUKE OF FLORENCE

VALENTIO DI' BUONDELMONTE

UBERTO, friend of Valentio

ODDO D'AMEIDEI

LAMBERTUCCIO D'AMEIDEI, brother of Oddo

BEATRICE, daughter of Lambertuccio

RINIERI, LUCIO, SCHIATTO { .... Friends of Lambertuccio & Oddo

LORENZO, FRANCESCO, BERNARDO { .... Relatives of Lambertuccio & Oddo

ALDRUDA, widow of FORESE DI' DONATI, friend of Lambertuccio

LIVIA, daughter of Aldruda

TOMASSO, servant of Aldruda

STEFANO, servant of Livia

PILGRIM

Scene: Florence, 1215 AD

Part One

ACT I

Scene: A Public Square in Florence

[*Enter three* CITIZENS]

1ST CITIZEN [*to* 2ND CITIZEN, *who is silent*]: Now, now, why are you so silent? What disturbing thoughts have robbed you of speech?

2ND CITIZEN: Nay, fears that lie deeper than the sounding of words.

1ST CITIZEN: Come man; surely you mean not one of those petty fears which ever dye your cheeks with a sickly hue!

2ND CITIZEN: I heartily wish it were so. But wait; has it not reached your ears what has sped a few days past? 'tis now the general talk of Florence.

3RD CITIZEN: Mean you the broil betwixt the Ameidei and Uberto and his friend Valentio?

2ND CITIZEN: No other.

1ST CITIZEN: Well, well; broils, what else? This sound is new to my ears.

2ND CITIZEN: Lend them to me, then, and I'll repeat to you what imperfect knowledge has been carried to mine by the

Valentio Di'Buondelmonte

wind of rumour. For reasons not known (though some alleged it to be no more than the heat of the occasion) which methink must have been deeply rooted in his heart, nourished by passing time: a concealed hate that clad in words gave vent to itself, Oddo (a youth full fiery and bold) flung hot insults in Uberto's furious face in the midst of a banquet gathering the Flower of the town, whilst in noisy merriment and lavish feasting where the gilded cups were never emptied of golden wine. . . . Uberto, impatient of the insult, restrained not his wounded pride from answering back in sharpest terms; whereupon Oddo, replying with his sword assailed the unexpecting youth, and would surely have slain him, had not Valentio, with friendly rage, and with eager arm forced Odd's sword to miss its mark; nay, more, he carved a deep gash in Odd's frame, and would have added more had he not deemed it answer enough to Oddo's arrogance. Hereupon the banquet was drawn into two and a general fight might have concluded, and God wot what noble blood might have flowed that day, had not some more sober among them scattered the aroused parties. I know no more. But my scarce knowledge is a rich foreboding of a tempest drawing nigh which will hurl its thunderbolts on our reposing town and burn it with Hellish fire.

3RD CITIZEN: Your fears are no baseless fancy-fabric. Foul rumours (more foul than their begetters) infest the startled air: Oddo's kin, 'tis claimed, declining bloodless terms, are banding themselves and drawing to them their scattered forces, and many a friendly house in Florence looks with favouring eyes on these matters.

1ST CITIZEN: 'Tis hard indeed for my credulence to grant this strange news; my fancy revolts to figure these peaceful streets made a bloody battlefield.

2ND CITIZEN: Amen! [*to* 3RD CITIZEN] And in what manner has the Duke welcomed the news?

Act I

3RD CITIZEN: 'Tis not yet known. But he's our only hope. Let's pray that he will prevent this coming woe, that these foul rumours may seem the idle inventions of overwrought brains, with no more substance of truth than a dream. *Exeunt*

[*Enter* ODDO, LAMBERTUCCIO, *and* RINIERI]

LAMB. [*to* ODDO]:
Of thy new broil, which adds one more to the
Quick-swelling number of thy foolish deed
I'm well informed, and Florence echoes it;
What's graver yet, that thou art minded
Of bitter strife and bloody commerce,
And wouldst not espouse fair Peace.

ODDO:
Fair Peace!
'Twere fair indeed wedded to downcast-eyed
Disgrace! Thy words fall on my startled ear
Like sounds from some strange land; that, thou should'st know
Being of D'Ameidei's blood, as I; but 'tis not strange
To thee since they're thy lips that are guilty.
Peace, how dearly bought, when purchased with
The coins of shame!

RINIERI:
Disgrace there's naught; for it
Dwells not with valour, whose right arm thou art;
Rather 'twill be made known that 'tis but through
Disdain to strike and not through fear that thou
Returnest not Valentio's blows with like [*after a pause*]
Though even if thou didst truly fear to rouse
His kin, whose name makes half of Florence
Tremble, thy valour's sheen would not be dulled.

LAMB.:
Most wisely said; and yet, thou wrongest us

Valentio Di'Buondelmonte

By doubt; were our cause just, naught could make us
Decline the field though all the powers of Hell
Were to oppose us. But with Valentio
Doth justice abide, and to him Justice
Shall be administered. Then is not Peace
The least we can offer?

Oddo:

Name not again
That hateful word which falls like to the screech
Of night's foul bird on my enraged ear,
And makes my blood seethe in my throbbing veins.

Lamb.:

Thou speakest not words by sober reason tamed;
O wilt then have Florence aflame with war?
(Thou canst not be ignorant how it unloosens
The chained might of Evil, marring
The beauty of the world with blood and fire,
Making of it a Hell, where it should be
A human Paradise) and shall we fight
Betwixt ourselves and let the envious foes
Of happy Florence be merry at her woe?
This incident is of light consequence:
Leave it to time, 'twill heal both wounds alike.

Oddo:

Bid me forget all things dear to my heart,
And all the joys of life, yea life itself,
And lie in a cold tomb and rot; but not
That bold outrage that left the eloquent mark
Of its mockery on my revolting frame
An everlasting stain, exposed to scorn,
Traced by pointing fingers, which when point not
Eyes cry: "Behold the white-cheeked coward"!
Rinieri [*aside, reflecting on* Oddo's *last words*]
Poor Honour, how I pity thee, since thou

Act I

Hast naught save wavering opinion
To nourish thee, and thou art swayed by the
Caprice of mere men, and by every blast
Of various thought; aye, thou art miserable!
I would not have thee in my company. [*to* LAMB. *and* ODDO]
Let's to the Duke, since you're at variance;
Whose sound and noble mind hath earned him fame
Like Israel's old sceptered sage; for their Justice
His mild domain unfurls.

ODDO [*aside*]:
To that old fool! [*in a loud voice*]
Aye, to demand justice, denied me here,
But if I find it not, I'll seek it elsewhere. *Exeunt.* [ODDO *stays behind, muttering between his teeth*]:
Thou shalt escape me not, for all *their* words. [*Exit* ODDO]

[*Enter* DUKE *of Florence, attended by his retinue,* FLOURISH.]

DUKE [*aside*]:
O most unhappy Florence; how soon the somber
Shadows of dire destruction threaten
To fall again on thy life's sunny way
And bleach the rosy cheeks with pallid fear,
Repeating for the hundredth time the sorry
Tale in its bloody history. O Sodom
Doomed to be dyed for e'er with running gore,
Thy silent streets for ever haunted by
The specter of death, and they great palaces
The banquet-halls of reveling Mars!
O for these haughty slaves whose hearts rejoice
In civil blood, rather than to unsheathe
Their eager words in the stern faces
Of Florence's common foes; while I am doomed
To play a poor spectator's sorry part
Possessing not the power to do aught else,
Compelled to taste the bitterness to be

Valentio Di'Buondelmonte

In name the ruler, in power not.
But could I force the fleeting years retrace
Their dusty steps, regain the heart unflinching
And stout, of youth, pour ardour warm and zeal
Herculean might to my sore trembling arms,
I would not linger here uttering vain words.
O idle wish bred of impotency!
What redress doth remain save to assay
To reconcile the alienated hearts?

[*Re-enter* Oddo, Lamb., Valentio, *and* Rinieri]

Oddo [*addressing the* Duke]:

My Lord, I come demanding that Justice
Be done to me.

Duke:

Hast thou been wronged?

Oddo:

Aye, wronged,
Abused, scorned in the midst of gentlemen,
And made a Justice-seeking fool, the while
The root and source of all that roameth free
Like as the fowls of heaven, and perchance
To my undoing.

Duke:

Thou awakenest
My curiousness to learn the name of the bold
Offender: pray how goes it?

Oddo:

A name
My furious lips would scorch if they assay
To spell it: 'tis no stranger to your ear.

Act I

RINIERI:
　It spells 'Valentio,' Your Highness.

[*Enter* VALENTIO *and* UBERTO]

DUKE:
　Ah here he comes. [*to* VALENTIO] This gentleman [*pointing to* ODDO] doth claim
　Amends for certain wrongs that he maintains
　Thou hast done him. How wouldst thou defend
　Thyself against this charge?

VALENTIO [*after a pause*]:
　My silence, both
　With his wound plead him right.

UBERTO:
　Not so, my Lord,
　'Tis I, not he who needs should suffer Thy wrath.

VALENTIO:
　Nay, heed him not, my Lord; he speaks
　Thus, driven by a generous nature.

DUKE [*to* VALENTIO *and* UBERTO]:
　Verrily
　I marvel greatly at your words: I have
　Not seen before this day men enamoured
　So much to punishment! I do commend
　Your noble friendship, but yet I demand
　To know who the offender is.

VALENTIO:
　'Tis I.

UBERTO:
　Nay, 'tis I.

Valentio Di'Buondelmonte

DUKE [*reflecting*]:
>Since each of you would fain
>So firmly bear the charge and doth abide
>Unshaken in his judgment, it meseems
>Well to devise some other way to extricate
>Us from this difficulty. [*to* LAMB.] A daughter fair
>Hast thou, if I am well informed: a maid
>More fair than heaven's sun, but not a whit
>Less scorching, whom I did behold one day
>Happier than any in my life, and so
>Surpassing fair was she that amorous Time,
>Wounded by the darts of Love fled with haste
>Lest he be wounded more, that I knew not how;
>And she made ma sore rune my palsied age
>And envy most bold youth.

LAMB. [*bowing low*]:
>My Lord, you flood
>My humble self with all this generous praise,
>Beyond all hope of thanks I abide
>In debt.

DUKE:
>She's called Beatrice, is it not so?

UBERTO [*aside, with his hand on his heart*]:
>Hush, fond heart,
>Thou makest me believe it was her name I heard!

ODDO [*aside, impatiently*]:
>The devil, the Duke turned out a doting lover!

DUKE:
>Most becoming name for one who doth
>Have eyes that make the jealous Queen of Night
>To quit with shame and heaven's lights burn out
>Themselves with spite.

Act I

UBERTO [*aside*]:
> Of her he must be speaking, since to whom
> Other than her can this description fit.
> But yet I fear my ears do play me false,
> Or I awake in an idle dream
> With semblance of reality.

DUKE:
> She is
> A virgin rose but newly blown from the bud.
> 'Tis seemly that the amorous butterflies
> Should woo her from her maiden dreams.

LAMB.:
> Mean you
> My Lord: that she should marry?

DUKE:
> Aye, that I meant.

UBERTO [*aside*]:
> O joy! What glorious hope doth swell from out the dark
> Deeps of my heart, like as the glorious break of day
> After a weary night; and yet I dare not
> Cherish it for long, and feed it with my
> Slumbering dreams lest its life's span
> Be brief even as it is glorious.

LAMB.:
> To whom,
> My Lord

DUKE:
> Why, to Valentio;
> And the gall of hatred will pass away
> Like as a summer cloud.

Valentio Di'Buondelmonte

ODDO [*aside, angrily*]:
> By Beelzebub!
> A lunatic would not utter such a damned outrage! [*aloud*]
> My Lord, surely you are but jesting, though
> I must avow it doth amuse me not.

UBERTO [*aside*]:
> Great heavens! heard you all this? No, No,
> It cannot be! What man would steal my Love
> From me; no not my friend! My wrought fancy
> Is fooling me. Aye, 'tis my fancy.
> [*tries to laugh, but it sounds hollow, and he starts*]
> But wherefore
> My laugh sounds so, and wherefore do I start?

DUKE [*to* ODDO]:
> Why dost thou marvel; 'tis very simple. [*to* VALENTIO] What
> Sayst thou?

VALENTIO:
> My thanks to Your Highness for your
> Most generous offer; but whether I do
> Espouse a maiden fair or else a colder Fate
> 'Tis one to me; nay, if any of the gentlemen
> Doth wish, by reason of aught whate'er,
> To th' contrary of what Your Highness
> Did propose, 'tis my desire to bear your wrath
> And punishment than be mistook
> For some wife-sheltered coward.

DUKE [*turning to* LAMB. *and* ODDO]:
> What say you?

LAMB.:
> I'm of your mind, Your Highness.

ODDO:
> I'm not—you're murdering Justice!

Act I

LAMB.:
> Nay, it is
> My private right to grant consent, or to
> Refrain. [*to* RINIERI]
> What thinkest thou?

RINIERI:
> 'Tis proper that
> He doth espouse thy daughter.
> [*in an undertone*] He seems
> A worthy gentleman.

VALENTIO:
> My Lord, I . . . .

DUKE [*interrupting him*]:
> No more protests!

ODDO:
> You band yourselves
> 'Gainst me. I shall abide it no more. [*aside, looking at Buondelmonte with flaming eyes and clenched fist*]
> Thou hast again escaped me: and with
> A beautiful bride! Blessed Sleep, visit no more
> These burning eyes, and O light-hearted Ease,
> Forsake my breast till I do quaff the sweet
> Wine of Revenge to the last dregs. [*Exits*]

DUKE [*to* VALENTIO, *who is pensive*]:
> Why, thou dost look like to a lover
> Hopeless in his love. Clouded brows befit
> No bridegroom; certes not for such a bride!

RINIERI:
> He marvels at his good fortune, methinks.

DUKE:
> Aye, that he should, in due order; but first
> Appoint a day to pledge his troth.

Valentio Di'Buondelmonte

LAMB.:
>Presently Your Highness. [*going*]

RINIERI [*whispers in* LAMB.*'s ear*]:
>Told thee not the Duke is wise? [*Exeunt*]

ACT II

Scene: A Room in Lambertuccio's Castle

As the curtain rises Beatrice is discovered pacing the room excitedly

BEATRICE:
    The sands have all run out, and still he tarries.
    O what can make him so belated? I
    Do fear some mishap hath befallen him.
    [*She stops suddenly and listens*]
    Can it be his footsteps?
    [*finds that there was no sound*]
    Troubled minds do thwart
    The natural offices of Nature. [*She continues to pace the room*]
    O if he comes not?
    [*Several taps are heard. She rushes to the door*]
    It is he at last! [*Opens the door*]

UBERTO:
    [*still outside, cautiously protrudes his head inside*]
    Art thou alone?

BEATRICE:
    Yea, have no fears;
    Father's out and the maid is on an errand. [UBERTO *enters*]

Valentio Di'Buondelmonte

My love, how cruel thou art to tarry
So long! Methought that lovers do possess
More gentle hearts. But no: the fire of Love
Within thy breast must have expired, or else
How couldst thou buy aught else with the dear price
Of Love's joy.

UBERTO:

Let the warmth of my kisses
Rather prove that it hath waxed stronger,
Or if thou wilt but put thy hand unto
My heart and feel how it doth throb for thee.
But no! Its fire would surely scorch thy hand.
And this is wherefore Love hath led me
Hither, to lull it smart into the lap
Of Sleep, with thy soft looks, though soon, alack
To wake again with greater might. For oh!
The cause of this my ailment is my cure,
Like to that brazen serpent that God's chosen
People erected in the sandy ocean. [*kisses her*]

BEATRICE:

O if this kiss could live forever, that I
May cling to it and thus, remain in changeless
Bliss amidst capricious Fate's Eternal
Inconstancy; or gazing into the Love-lit
Depths of thy dark eyes, to plunge in their
Infinitude until the very same
Abode of thy chaste soul, and with it
Mingle, and forget, as in the silent stream
Of Lethe, fears more dark than silent nights,
Conjured before my eyes in all shapes horrid.
For lived we not those holy moments
Stolen from the angels? (Not many may
More attain), then what remains to us
(Save death, to hold them back from Fate's
Eternal thievery) than decline dire

ACT II

And suffering if not estrangement?

UBERTO:
>Dear love, what wayward thoughts have slid into
>Thy beautiful little head! How can light
>And darkness dwell together in thy heart?
>Thy fears are fancy-woven; and what reward
>Have we to strain our weakling eyes in vain
>Essay to pierce the mist of the morrow?
>Let us enjoy the heaven-sent bliss ere 'tis
>Too late.

BEATRICE:
>'Tis only wise to fear the tempest
>When the sea doth seems most calm. O why
>Doth Heav'n reserve the bitterest Cup to lovers?

UBERTO:
>To put to proof their constancy; which if
>They bear with constant minds and changeless passion
>Grants them Bliss Eternal in Unity
>Unseverable, though sometimes after
>They do cast off their earthly raiment; and
>Besides, dear lady, only dolour great
>Brings forth great happiness: they go together;
>For are not roses by their thorns made fair?

BEATRICE [*noticing that he is paler than usual*]:
>The thorns of Love did start to pierce thy heart
>Methinks, or else why hast thou grown more pale?

UBERTO:
>My paleness is but the reflex of thy fears. [*footsteps are heard outside*]

BEATRICE [*agitated*]:
>My father! Hide behind the curtain.

Valentio Di'Buondelmonte

UBERTO:
> Nay, let me hide where I may revel yet
> Upon thy loveliness my famished eyes:
> I can endure not losing sight of thee.

BEATRICE:
> Quick, no more. [UBERTO *hides. Enter* LAMB.]:

LAMB.:
> I bring thee joyful news, Daughter, that
> Will revive (I hope) thy drooping and withering
> Petals; which less-knowing men would charge
> To Love's intemperate beams. But well
> I know that thou art wise and wouldst not
> Expose thyself to them, like foolish Youth
> That for it languisheth.

BEATRICE:
> 'Tis well and good if it can work such magic.

LAMB.:
> Thou art versed (in no way worse
> Than many a cloistered nun) in the
> Holy Scripts, how Man and Woman were
> Created twin trees with boughs entwined,
> Growing on the same soil and warmed by
> The selfsame sun, by the same breezes caressed . . .

BEATRICE [*impatiently*]:
> Indeed; and yet I do not see in this
> The good news.

LAMB.:
> Patience, daughter, let me
> Proceed. And since thou art a child no more
> It doth behoove thee to wed a gentleman
> Of gentle breed and culture; and thou art
> Most fortunate that such a winsome

ACT II

And handsome gentleman hath asked thy hand
And wishes to make thee a happy bride
Within the space of two days.

BEATRICE:
I myself
Have long ordained a bride to Christ within
The quiet walls of San Maggiore, and not
Unto a mortal man.

LAMB.:
Thou hast drawn little
From thy life's store, and therefore 'tis unwise
The richer treasure of the future
To lavish; which those whose store hath almost
Ran out can do without loss. Nay, 'tis e'en
A crime to cut off the warm sap of human
Joys from thy young and supple stem and cause
Thy new-blown blossoms of most lovely hue,
Which should delight a dainty eye to wither
Ere they bear fruit.

BEATRICE:
But father . . .

LAMB. [stopping her with a motion of his hand]

BEATRICE:
Suffer me to speak.

LAMB.:
Enough. [aside]
I should know women better. 'T's
Maiden coyness that doth make her speak
In such wise; and perchance a little
Of feminine art. [aloud] Tomasso! Tomasso!
[Enter Tomasso]

Valentio Di'Buondelmonte

TOMASSO:
>Thy pleasure, Sir?

LAMB.:
>Show thy skill, man, and deck
>The table with delicious dishes that
>Will invite a lusty appetite. [TOMASSO *bows and is retiring*]
>And forget
>Not the sparkling wine.
>[*Exit* TOMASSO]
>[*to* BEATRICE]
>Thy future husband and some of our old friends
>Are coming hither; therefore prepare thyself
>To meet them, and remember thy wedding. [*Exit* LAMB.]

BEATRICE:
>Woe, woe, without end or number! [UBERTO *comes out of hiding*]
>"Didst thou
>Hear?"

UBERTO:
>Alas, if hearing were but all! Say rather: "Didst
>Thou feel it? Did the accents rush upon
>Thy wounded ear with all the loosened might
>Of thunder, shaking thy inmost fibers
>And nerves and working havoc with thy soul, as armed
>With lightning's might electric. Did the ground
>Tremble beneath thy feet, as though to gape
>And hide thee in its earthy bowels from
>The woe to come? And yet, alack! This all
>Was but the augmentation of the bleeding
>Of a wounded heart; for I did carry
>The heavy burden of knowledge all the time"

BEATRICE [*talks to herself passionately in a loud voice*]:
>Accursed be the sinews that could bear

ACT II

Woe after woe and sorrow hand in hand
With brother sorrows! 'Twere best if they
Were crushed, as with the force of falling mountains,
Then 'twere the end of all, no more to bear.
But I must needs be doomed to further woes
Since I am able to endure so much. [*after a pause, slowly*]
He said he knew it all, but told me not
His love. Not e'en his eyes, no nor his voice
Betrayed the guarded secret. But instead
Led me astray with his false words, made mine
Prophetic fears an old wife's logic. Surely
He hath him banded with my father. No!
That heartless tyrant, that executioner. . . .
Forgive me Christ! O how came these unholy
Words to my lips, and from what profane
Recess! Did he not bring me hither? Yet
What doth *it* offer save salt tears and sighs?
'Twere better if these eyes knew not blessed light
Nor not these ears delighted in the lark's
Sweet song, or in the drowsy murmur
Of gliding streams.

UBERTO:

For the love of our Lord torment me
No more, dearest love. I bore the pain
Of the knowledge unshared, rather than
To grieve twice by causing thee to grieve.
[BEATRICE *breaks into nervous sobbing.* UBERTO *falls down on his knee beside her and takes her hand*]
There, there, Mignonne. Thou dost obscure thy eyes
So sunny, with these wintry clouds. [*She still weeps*]

TORRENTS:

Of tears wash not away a fixed sorrow:
They but submerge it. Let's therefore reserve
Them till having essayed to pluck it
We fail (if by ill-fate we fail). But now

Valentio Di'Buondelmonte

A greater quest doth lie before us:
To free us from the iron mesh that Fate
Hath warily entangled us in. [BEATRICE *has stopped sobbing*]

BEATRICE:

No ray of hope do I descry breaking
The darkness of despair. The snare is strongly
Woven, and what, alas, can startled deer
Contrive, to overcome the wariness
Of the hunter?

UBERTO:

Nay! Like to enraged lions
We shall force our way out of the pit.

BEATRICE:

And time doth fly with breathless haste! I would
The sun may ne'er forsake our darkened earth
But linger 'bout and keep perpetual day
That the morn of my wedding may never dawn.

UBERTO:

Unsay these words, beloved: thou shalt obey
Thy father's will and shalt espouse, yet none
Save me, and not in Florence, but in
Some happier town where we can freely draw
The lighter air of love. Thy look tells me
Thou didst not fathom yet my meaning; we
Shall steal from this accursed hell guided
By the midnight moon, who shall be also
Sole witness to our nuptials. Only steal
Thou from this house whilst all are steeped in Sleep's
Dulling potion, and thou shalt find me waiting.
And now farewell. [*turns to go*]

BEATRICE:

O stay! I'm sick and faint
Lest we shall meet no more strengthen me,

ACT II

Inspire me with thy stern purpose, that
I may be able to fulfill our resolve.

UBERTO:

Staying longer maketh parting more difficult.
We must needs fast our eyes on one another
For the space of tomorrow, but then we shall
Feast them for evermore.
Besides, I leave my heart with thee, thy
Eternal friend, who shall be thy support
With love's great might. [*Exit* UBERTO]

BEATRICE:

What strange events have sped
Before mine wondering eyes in but a day's
Brief span, beyond the ken of wildest fancy's
Flight! I must calmly think them o'er. [*Exit* BEATRICE]
[*Enter* ODDO, ALDRUDA, *and* LIVIA]

ODDO [*looking around him*]:

Meseems we are not welcome. But list!
What sayest thou to my proposal?

ALDRUDA:

My dull brain
Hath formed but a faint image of thy words,
Being slow to comprehend, by reason of
Advanced age.

ODDO:

Thou of a surety art
Well informed concerning Beatrice's shameful
Wedding, since it is a common knowledge by
This time, and so I need not tax thy ears
By saying it o'er, but repeating what else
I've said: albeit all efforts which I generously
Did lavish to avert the sacrifice of
The guiltless damsel on the altar of

Valentio Di'Buondelmonte

A selfish person's insolence have failed,
Still steadfastly bent on my intent, still fain
Would spare the powerless Lamb. from the wolf's
Hungry teeth and having thought of thee
As one most fit for the execution
Thereof, knowing the fertility
Of their cunning, I've hied to thee to lend
Me a helping hand. The vulture fierce masked by
A dove's soft plumes will soon alight in this
Calm nest to win his easy prey with feigned
Accents. It behooves thee therefore (if
My request hath found some favour in
Thy heart), to spread the snare such wise that no
Outlet is left to flee therefrom. But thy
Daughter's eyes [*gazing at* LIVIA] can well entangle him
In the foils of Love, methinks. [*Gives her a fat purse*] This will
Illume to thee my meaning better.

ALDRUDA [*with cold dignity*]:
    What, a fee?!

ODDO:
    A symbol of my great esteem for thee.
    But why duel in studied accents, since
    We know to foil each other's thrusts?
    Aldruda [*taking the purse from him. With dignity*] Thanks!

ODDO:
    I must needs leave you now, with hope of quick
    Success.

ALDRUDA:
    Aye, and abide with it until success
    Crown it with verity. [*Exit* ODDO]
    [*aside*] He speaks so well
    As to convince all those who know
    Him not of what he says. Yet what care I!
    Have I not mine ambition too? Such bridegrooms

ACT II

Fall not every day on one's way. And
'Tis I who have to hunt for bridegrooms
For her! [*nodding towards her daughter*] Whilst she, like as a
Recluse old, hath firmly locked the gates of her soul,
And hath not left e'en a window wherefrom light
May pass into that dark and silent abode
Or to commune with our corporeal earth,
Doth she (I wonder) not shiver in the cold
Night-dew when gazing the long, still hours
Onto the starless firmament of her soul,
And doth not fear creep through every
Channel and highway to her lonely heart
When the bleak silent winds do range on its
Desolate plains? Are there brooks and seas?
They must needs be silent, to match her own,
Methinks. [*aloud to* LIVIA] Get thee behind that door
[*points to a door in the middle back of the stage*]
And there
Abide until I open it to thee.

LIVIA:

Prithee to what
Purpose, madam?

ALDRUDA:

No matter for the moment;
Thou shalt know presently. [LIVIA *obeys*] [*Enter* VALENTIO]

VALENTIO:

Good evening madam.

ALDRUDA:

No greetings for him who doth accept a bride through fear.

VALENTIO:

Surely thou meanest me not, though thy words, meseems
Are otherwise meant. But were I so
Addressed I would reply that no man who is

Valentio Di'Buondelmonte

    A true knight would accept such an
    Dishonourable bargain.

ALDRUDA:

    Then by what manner
    Hast thou accepted Beatrice? Thou canst not
    Deny that 'twas through fear of the Duke's wrath
    Or else the swords of Di'Amediei.
    Leave her that thou wouldst take for wife; choose
    This damsel in her place, and be henceforth
    A brave and honoured gentleman.

VALENTIO:

    Believe me,
    Madam, thou hast not been informed aright,
    Besides . . .
    [ALDRUDA *stops him with her hand and throws open the chamber door, exposing* LIVIA]
    What heavenly vision is this!
    Were it not day I had thought it a dream,
    A mere shadow, an airy nothing. But
    Methinks, methinks mine eyes have alighted
    On this celestial form or in my dreams
    Prefiguring it, or ere I put on
    This mortal garb. Aye, I've beheld these eyes!
    These two bright orbs that like twin stars have since
    Shone in my heart. [*to* LIVIA] Speak, O Vision
    If thou beest acquainted with our earthly
    Manner of speech. But no, I do repent
    Me of my words; for thou art thus truer
    An angel, thy silence is far more
    Eloquent than all the arts of Orators.
    Livia [*to her mother*]
    I marvel yet what all these things may mean.

ALDRUDA:

    Ask thy heart: if it hath naught to say

ACT II

Only then will I speak. [LIVIA *blushes*]
Valentio [*to* ALDRUDA] Alas! 'Tis now too late.

ALDRUDA:

    Nay, thou
    Canst even yet have her: dare not to take
    The step and let the consequences rest
    On me?

VALENTIO:

    I do dare. [*steps forward and raises* LIVIA's *hand to his lips*]
    Let me seal my pledge with my lips. [*Enter* LAMB.]
    [*aside; startled*]
    O my God!

LAMB.

    Welcome, most welcome. [*to* ALDRUDA, *pointing towards* LIVIA]
    My friend lives yet in her noble features. [to LIVIA]
    Give me thy hand; it makes me feel the warmth
    Of youth. [*turning to* VALENTIO] The maid told me Beatrice is ill
    And so you will not see each other now:
    I know too well this will not please thee, but
    Perchance it is consoling that this
    Delayed joy will doubly be repaid
    When you will meet. [*to all*] Dinner is ready;
    Allow me to conduct you to it.

VALENTIO

    Waste not
    For me your leisure: I will follow soon.
    But first I have to ease me of some thoughts
    That claim immediate attention. [*Exeunt all except* VALENTIO]
    [VALENTIO *paces the stage for some time with apparent agitation.*
    The changes in his expression indicating that a struggle is going on
    within him. Suddenly he bursts out:]
    My God, oh, my God! . . . . . What! Crying
    To God with the same lips that ere long I did

Valentio Di'Buondelmonte

Forswear! O mockery of mockeries!
And will God heed my cry? No, no; my lips
Still savour of forswearing. Then to whom
Shall I cry? To the howling winds? My cry,
Outstripping their unbounded passion, will
Make them grow silent with fear. To the
Reposing mountains? Like a spasm o'er the whole
Wide earth my cry will startle them and they
Will shiver. To the heaving billows:
What boot when greater waves of warring Powers
Break on the shattered rocks of this poor heart.
[*places his hand on his heart*]
Nay, rather this vile heart that did violate
Hospitality in its own sanctuary!
No, but I will forswear my forswearing. What!
Add one forswearing more? No, no, the second
Pledge is null; 'twas no more mine to give it.
Besides, the weal of all Florence doth rest
On it, and shall I prove unworthy of the
Trust of my friends, forsooth a perjurer?
I must uproot this love that hath in such
Strange wise been planted in the frailest part
Of my heart, ere its fragile roots grow firm, and
Extend in its soft soil and fill it. But
Alack! Is it not cruel exceedingly? Nay,
The crown and masterpiece of cruelty
To break a guileless maiden's heart. To break
Her's breaks mine also, and what evil
Have I committed to deserve this?
To be compelled to strangle my first, young love
When 'tis but newly born? Why, yielding
To her like as a weakling child? Then, I
Had been carefree, an honorable man.
But wherefore censure my frail heart for loving?
What heart can the resistless battering
Of Love withstand? No, no, not when
Its darts come from such eyes! They would make Love

ACT II

Itself lovesick! Is it her fault, then? Nay;
Could she prevent her eyes from conquering,
And is not love made but for Youth: that lyre
Whose flowing numbers played by angelic fingers
It is; that rose whose scent it is.
Then shall I buy the wisdom of old age
By being false to Youth? Nay, I will none
Of it. I'd rather be a lover and a fool
Than a sage and loveless; rather
A loving enemy than a loveless friend,
And none shall durst call me afraid of the
Ameidei! Then why al this faltering,
All these vain words? If they want war, I am
Their man. Love will lead me to victory.
In what doth Honour lie? In serving Love.
In what doth Power, Truth, Right, Kingdom
Consist? In obeying the call of Love.
I did forswear unto a Duke? What then?
I pay homage unto a God! Let the Duke
Demand his pledge of him if he wish! [*Exit*]

ACT III

Scene: Front of Lambutuccio's castle
Time: Night

[*Enter* UBERTO]

UBERTO:
    How still is this serenest night! Now
    The whole wide world is fast intoxicated
    With the sparkling wine of gilded sleep.
    E'en the nocturnal bat reposes
    Whilst I, like to some portion of night's very self
    Steal through the dark, out-waking all, except
    The ever-sleepless host of the skies.
    [*Gazes at* BEATRICE'*s window which looks down on the street*]
    Her room
    Is wrapt in darkness; I do fear she too
    Hath drunk the wine of Lethe. Fain would I
    Wake her to my presence but for my fear
    To wake up foreign eyes. But patience, O
    My heart. Soon will she come and then, O bright
    And gentle moon . . . [*Lifts his eyes to the sky*]
    O no, he's pale and wan.
    What? May it be that thou art jealous that
    I am a happy lover, whilst thou wanderest

Valentio Di'Buondelmonte

Loveless in yon vast trackless void amidst
The alien stars that have no common bond?
For shame, deny this charge, say 'tis not true,
Thou friend to bards and lovers plaintive,
That lendest ever-heeding ears to their
Complaints and sighs, and growest pale and faint
With sympathy. Then lo! thou growest envious
When they do taste the joys of love repayed
With equal passion! It grieveth me
O moon to see thee grieve that I am glad.
I pray thee, gentle moon, brighten thy brow
So sullen, that thy light may guide my feet
In the path of bliss.
[*Enter* BEATRICE]

BEATRICE:

Thy love. But soft, whom have we here? [*Walks towards him*]

UBERTO [*stepping forward*]:

And thine. [*They embrace*]

BEATRICE:

Ah me! Thy lips are cold,
Cold as the winds of winter breaking through
The frozen air; O have the stars on their
Crimson petals distilled their cold night dew?

UBERTO:

The cold is naught whilst hearts be warm; fear only
When they are chilled with love dead. But no more now:
We must away. For lo! The betraying streaks
Of day from yonder Orient gates of Heaven
Do rend the velvet folds of friendly night.
Such is our present lot, beloved: the night
Of Care is giving way to radiant morn. The Sun
Of Love will shine on us and keep our hearts
Aflame, and will not set until our mortal
Day be o'er.

ACT III

BEATRICE:

> Nay, Love; pray that it may
> Remain a torch beyond the gloom of Death.
> Let us pray, and let greedy Oblivion
> The past devour. [*Exeunt. Enter a* PILGRIM]

PILGRIM:

> The diligent sun hath begun to rise from his fleecy bed of clouds to start afresh his daily course; but this day he will not plod alone, with worn-out feet his ever-trodden way in the deserted heavens. I shall be his fellow-traveler though our goals be different: his, the western abode beyond the distant mountains, mine, Rome. But God alone knows full well how many times he will traverse the skies ere I behold myself without the gates of Rome. Rome! Queen of the Capitals of the world and mother to all Christendom; the treasure-casket of the hallowed bones of the antique saints who lived and died there and sanctified the very stones on which they trod and the air they breathed. I will walk where the Great Caesars once walked, amidst the huge marble pillars and statues carved by dexterous hands, that remain eternal and eloquent, though silent witnesses of the Splendour that once was. I will pray for forgiveness in blessed Peter's Church and also in the Church of St. Lorenzo, my patron saint. I will fall on my knees before the Holy Father and kiss his holy feet and he will bless me; and when the day of Our Lord's rising be o'er, I'll betake me back cleansed of all sins, a righteous man of God.
> [*Enter* BEATRICE's *maid from the castle, going in the opposite direction*]

PILGRIM:

> Good-morrow, Lady.

MAID:

> Good-morrow, Sir.

Valentio Di'Buondelmonte

PILGRIM:

Why, roses ope not their folded petals till the sunbeams kiss them. By our Lady, you'll make the sun ashamed to rise, seeing that you're more pretty than she.

MAID:

Are your words, Sir, true interpreters of your thoughts?

PILGRIM:

God forbid that they should be otherwise. My grey hairs and my vocation witness to their truth: *Fructus sciet arboris.*

MAID:

Thank you Sir; but in what tongue was it that last you spoke?

PILGRIM:

The tongue of the Apostles, saints and friars. [*aside*] Doubtless Christ too spoke it.

MAID:

You should be one of them you mentioned, to speak it.

PILGRIM:

I'm but a poor pilgrim.

MAID:

You are very humble, Sir.

PILGRIM [*gazing at the house*]:

Who dwells within these grim battlements and strong walls?

MAID:

The lion is known from his den; why, the great
And noble Lambertuccio D'Ameidei, my Lord. But oh, I well-nigh forgot: my lady his daughter, will wed today; we have preparations to make; so I fear me I have to leave you sir. [*Looks towards the castle's entrance as though in fear*]

ACT III

PILGRIM:
> D'Ameidei! Why, that's a happiness not bestowed on everyone; and a wedding too! That's still greater. [*aside*] I wish my journey were not today, then I had attended it. [*aloud*] Greetings to your lady and my wishes to you for an early wedding.

MAID:
> Oh, sir, you're very kind!

PILGRIM:
> Kindness is a quality of God Himself; but let me not delay you longer. Good day.

MAID:
> Good day, good pilgrim, and remember me in your prayers.
> [*Exit* PILGRIM]
> [*Enter* TOMASSO *as maid is going in the opposite direction*]

MAID [*smiling*]:
> Good morrow, master Tomasso.

TOMASSO:
> Good morrow. But what may't be that you greeted me in this fashion contrary to thy usual manner?

MAID [*scolding*]:
> Why, master Tomasso, your words surprise me. Greet I you not every morn with the best courtesy in the world, in no way worse than gentle-bred ladies.

TOMASSO:
> Aye, there's no denial to that; but you are false to thy nature in being gay.

MAID [*annoyed*]:
> Better than be false to a wedding-day. [*turns to go*]

Valentio Di'Buondelmonte

TOMASSO:

> There, there! Lay not my words to heart, if I desired to have thee false to the wedding, I myself would be false to it, while I am glad with all my heart for it.

MAID [*slyly*]:

> O, you are becoming . . .

TOMASSO [*eagerly*]:

> For God's sake out with it; my very breath hangs on it.

MAID:

> As gentlewomen say: impertinent!
> [*Embarrassed,* TOMASSO *is at a loss for an answer. The maid laughs at his embarrassment. The voice of* LAMB., *from the castle*]
> Tomasso! Tomasso! [LAMB. *is seen standing on threshold of the door*]

LAMB. [*to* TOMASSO]:

> Come man, 'tis not the time for old-wife's tale;
> We've much to do, and the bridegroom will soon arrive.

TOMASSO:

> Aye, sir. [LAMB. *and* TOMASSO *go into the house. Maid shrugs and follows them*]

LUCIO [*Enter* LUCIO, SCHIATTI, *and* RINIERI. *Enthusiastically*]:

> How full of warm delight are wedding-days,
> When Nature seems dressed in her best attire
> Like to a bride adorned for her wedding;
> As though she fain would share and multiply
> A thousand-fold the joys of her young daughters'
> Nuptials! Behold the sky, cloudless and bright
> Like as the laughing eyes of a child, and lo!
> The whole wide world doth seem intoxicated
> With her own sweet beauty.

ACT III

SCHIATTI:
> Nuptials
> Present no joys for me save for the nectar
> Distilled from the juicy golden grape and stored
> In ancient caskets in the Earth's dark womb,
> To quench our earthly thirst, and so to drown
> Our souls in its purple ocean that they
> May e'er remain drenched with its warm dew
> Intoxicating, dreaming of lovely
> Lasses with star-like eyes and lips more sweet
> Than honey-dew that these soft Naiads
> With wings light-dusted sip.

LUCIO [*to* SCHIATTI]:
> Thou should'st have
> Been born in juicy Bacchus' revels
> To dote so much on wine!

RINIERI:
> And have the lasses
> Also a season of their own?

LUCIO:
> Aye,
> The youthful Spring, the bridal-time of the year,
> For then do roses blow, and violets shy,
> Lilies pure as a virgin's soul, and daffodils,
> Wild Nature's darlings wan, pale stars of the fields.

SCIATTI:
> Need I be born in generous Autumn,
> Or in the merry month of May, to have
> A thirst for wine and women? Youth, even
> Life is an infinite thirst that may not
> Be quenched, like love that no satiety
> Of sipping nectar from Love's flower knows:
> The Poet hath a thirst for loveliness

Valentio Di'Buondelmonte

In cloud and flower, wave and viewless thought,
And so therein lies his delight; the sage
Doth have a thirst for wisdom, and he seeks
To quench it; some have thirst for yellow gold,
An insane thirst some times, and they pursue
This selfsame end with minds and hearts attuned
To it. All men possess their own; let me
Have mine!

LUCIO:

But if this thirst may not be quenched
What boot to toil and sweat for it in vain?
Better that we assay to strangle it
In its frail infancy, than to cause us
Fever and suffering when it grows up.

SCHIATTI:

Aye,
These are true words by my faith ... [*Enter* LAMB.]

LAMB.:

Welcome friends!
You honour me as rarely as the rain
Visits the thirsty desert! How dost
Thou fare, Lucio; and thou, Rinieri?
How 'bout thee, friend Schiatti? Art thou still
Doting on wine?

LUCIO [*smiles*]:

Schiatti, like a true
And constant lover ne'er forgets his love.
He made it known to us ere long how fain
He was to have again her company.

LAMB.:

She's good, if she becometh not one's master
And thereby urge him to what becometh not
A man. But this day she shall be our host,

ACT III

To entertain our merry fancies light
With generous joys and make us shun the use
Of sober reason, and by outward deeds
Belie our outward semblance. [*Enter* ODDO]

ODDO:

What means
This gathering? Hath aught unnatural
Befallen you? [*pretending to remember*] Ah, the wedding;
Forgive my memory that holds its mirror
Imperfectly before my mind [*talking half to himself*]
Surely
He will prefer a bride for fetters, or
Exile! Indeed, to wed a person
By threats and frowns; the wildest fancy of a
Distracted mind is not so strange a thing!

LAMB.:

Thy words remind me thou dost harbour yet
A darkness in thy heart. I had well-nigh
Forgot it. But remember, soon will I
Enthrone him in my heart, like as a second
Love, beside the first: his present
Betrothed and his future wife; or like
A newborn son not of the flesh, but of
The soul; for what becometh one with Beatrice
Becometh one with me. Remember this
Also: he will become a brother to thee.

ODDO:

Nay, a nephew!

RINIERI [*trying to change the subject*]:

We're like a soul-forsaken
Body without the bride. Pray how fares she?

LAMB.:

The lazy bride! The morning light hath yet

Valentio Di'Buondelmonte

Not kissed her slumbering eyes, methinks she must
Be loath to be disturbed from her sweet dreams.

LUCIO:

Soon she'll arise from those sweet dreams to sweeter
Reality, and then she would fain keep
Awake for e'er.

LAMB.:

Sublime reality:
When dressed in her white gown (a lily
Enfolded in her lily-leaves], perchance
The angels will descend from Heaven to join
The ceremony, mistaking her for one
Of their throng. [*the* MAID *passes. To the* MAID:]
Wake up thy lady; she hath
O'erslept herself. [MAID *goes into the house*]
[*Re-enter* MAID *after a while, crying*]

MAID:

Ah me! The lady! O woe! The lady!

LAMB.:

What means your wailing thus?!

MAID:

Oh the lady, the lady Beatrice is gone; O woe, woe! She's gone!

ODDO:

She seems distracted from her wits by some
Strange sorrow. [*to the* MAID] How now, woman,
Explain!

MAID:

She's not in her bed; the bed is cold—she's nowhere; O the lady!

ACT III

SCHIATTI:
> Enough! [*all rush into the house. All reenter with* TOMASSO]

LAMB.:
> O Beatrice, Beatrice! O cruel
> Cruel name! It makes my lips to bleed
> When they breathe it! No more Beatrice to greet
> My heart with her sweet voice! She's fled like as
> A brief, brief dream—Oh doth a dream return?
> More cruel question. The only star that burnt
> In the eternal night of my lone soul
> Is no more! Accursed Fate, that hast
> Made mine unwilling eyes to witness
> My daughter, yea, the very flesh and blood
> Of me, leave me in the autumn of
> My life to face alone the frosty winds
> Of winter, and descend unlamented
> Into the eternal grave. O why hath death
> Not visited me ere this hath come to pass,
> That I might have surrendered me to his
> Embrace, and pressed his frozen lips to mine?
> Then I would have been spared this torture:
> Torture worse than death; for is not
> A hope-deserted man but walking-death,
> A ruined castle through whose prostrate pillars
> No breeze of hope doth blow; the very
> Incarnation of Misery! O that
> She's been a mother; then surely she would
> Not have forsaken me! [*A tear rolls down his cheek*] Unmanly
> Intruder, thou wouldst not have dared to swell
> In these proud eyes that have made many a
> Stout-hearted for to tremble, but that
> I bear within my breast a father's womanly
> Heart. Ah me, that such a gentle maid
> As thou, shouldst wound my heart more sorely than
> The sharpest swords of foes!

Valentio Di'Buondelmonte

SCHIATTI:
> Compose thyself.
> What boot to linger and lament our mishaps
> Rather than seek to remedy them?
> Lame grief but chills the willing hand of action.

LAMB.:
> Thou hast not been a father, friend . . .

ODDO [*to* SCHIATTI]:
> Thou speakest
> Aright. We must to action. [*to* TOMASSO] Get ready
> The swiftest horses in the stable, and
> Prepare thyself for a human chase. [TOMASSO *starts to* go]
> Tarry
> A little. [*turning to the others*]Wherefore gaze you all silently
> In one another's face as seeking council?
> Will no one offer his powers for seeking Beatrice?
> But remember that she must have stolen
> With some lover. He may be desperate—
> Let him who doth desire to go look to
> His sword.

LUCIO & Schiatti [*together*]: We are thy men.

ODDO:
> Well then,
> Council among thyselves who will to Pisa,
> Who to Rome, and who to Venice.
> Put now to horse and bear in mind not to
> Return save with Beatrice.
> [*Exeunt* TOMASSO, LUCIO, *and* SCHIATTI *hurriedly*]

RINIERI [*musing on what happened*]:
> Great God, how she
> Deserted him! And why? Was she in love? Loved
> She not her father? What, love wars with love?!
> Most horrible war! All this in the gentle

ACT III

Bosom of Beatrice, silently and with
No outward mark! Lightning should have convulsed
The face of the heavens; thunder, his herald,
Borne on the wings of the swift winds should have
Proclaimed the civil strife in the four corners
Of the world and the vast seas should have swelled
And roared with indignation.
But lo, the war is done, too soon, alas,
And lo, behold the vanquished father, yoked
With tears and embittered memories. Cruel Fate,
That Man should reap the thorns of sorrow for
Sown love. [*Enter* LORENZO, FRANCESCO, *and* BERNARDO]

LORENZO:

No longer tax your patience to keep alive
The dying beams of expectation in
Your eyes: if I guess right the bridegroom will
Be with us soon. We beheld him enter
The house of Di Donati.

FRANCESCO:

Aye, not long
Ago, whilst we were on our way hither.

BERNARDO:

His feet scarce seemed to touch the ground, though
By nimble spirits borne; or that he
Did fear lest he doth tread too hard upon
His Mother Earth, and by great joy to cause
Her pain.

FRANCESCO:

His every motion seemed in sweet
Accord with inward harmony. Even
The living air he seemed to fill with the
Fragrance of joy.

BERNARDO:

One could wax happy in

His happiness, to see his brimful eyes
Reflect the fire that glowed within his heart
Deepening the crimson hue of his cheeks: he was indeed
A very Poet in rapturous frenzy.

FRANCESCO:

I trow he saw us not for oblivious joy.

ODDO [*aside*]:

Bravo Aldruda! My confidence
Was not misplaced. The darling robin
Hath been entangled in thy daughter's
Enticing beams more easily than I
Dared to forecast. But rest assured, he shall
Remain not long in thy possession! [*Aloud, pretending indifference*] I
Fear me you have to summon all your
Powers of patience, contrary to what
Lorenzo would have it.

FRANCESCO [*to* ODDO]:

Wherefore? Dost thou
Suspect a fraud?

RINIERI:

There is naught
To suspect. He needs must have gone thither
To accompany Lady Aldruda hither.

ODDO [*sarcastically*]:

Why not Livia?

LORENZO:

Why dally we in barren
Arguments? Soon will we know the truth.
If he means to observe his pledge shortly
He must be here.

ACT III

BERNARDO [*to* LAMB.]:
> What hour was fixed for the
> Wedding?

RINIERI:
> That hour was left behind some time
> Ago. Yet it is useless now to speak
> Of perjury (if haply he foreswears
> His troth) after the mishap that
> Befell us.

ODDO:
> Away with thy painted logic!
> Pour it in coward ears to match their listening
> Fear, and not into the ears of those
> Of the Ameidei sprung.

LAMB. [*to* ODDO]:
> The charge is yet
> Unproved. Assay not in vain to seduce
> Me to the use of arms. He hath been till
> This very day an honorable gentleman.

ODDO:
> Thy eyes must needs be dim not to behold
> The dazzling truth! unlawful eyes do hold
> In thralldom his inconstant heart. If thou
> Dost falter yet I needs must own that sorrow
> Hath stolen thy manliness!

BERNARDO:
> By God, then he
> Shall curse the day that he was born!

LORENZO:
> He will have a hard time from us, I swear!

Valentio Di'Buondelmonte

FRANCESCO:

> Death to the perjurer! [*Excited, they speak simultaneously, so that only a confused mixture of oaths and threats is heard*]

LAMB.:

> Peace, peace, my friends!
> Let us talk more calmly. [*the others, not listening to* LAMB. *Together*]
> Death to the perjurer!

LAMB. [*resigned*]:

> Be it as you will. [*Very coldly*] Bring me my sword.

ODDO [*to* LAMB.]:

> Thou needst
> Not trouble thee with this affair; leave it
> To me: my sword is eager to meet his.

LAMB. [*Suddenly in a sad voice*]:

> Thou shalt fight but a human foe, whilst I
> Must needs fight foes more dangerous far; foes that
> Make one to start from gentle sleep and molten
> Fire to scorch his flesh! Foes not without
> But within; myself against itself divided:
> Myself mine enemy. And this my heart
> The battlefield. [*Recovering his calmness*] Thou shalt fight him
> Man to man, sword to sword. So shalt thou have no
> Foul play, but honourable combat. Now I must
> Retire to my own self; to darksome silence:
> Shade born of darkness to shade born of light,
> To seek some peace. [*Exit* LAMB.]

ODDO [*aside*]:

> My brother pays
> Too slavish homage to empty rules. What!
> My life endanger again and face the Devil's
> Sword! No foul play! Ha, ha! He

ACT III

Shall have a dozen daggers stick in his
Soft hide, the churl!

RINIERI:

I've no more here. [*Exit*]

ODDO [*to* LORENZO]:

Knowest thou
A dagger's use?

LORENZO:

And more!

ODDO [*to* BERNARDO]:

And thou?

BERNARDO:

And a Mace too! Francesco and I.

ODDO:

Well then, I need your skill.
Let us proceed, and I'll unfold to you
my mind. [*Exeunt*]

ACT IV

Scene: Ponte Vecchio, Florence Easter
Time: Morning, 1215

Conspirators concealed within the courts and towers of the Ameidei.

Enter two citizens dressed in holiday clothes

1ST CITIZEN: I wish our good Lord had risen oftener. It had done us a great good, who find scarce an hour to draw lightly the free air and stretch our aching sinews in easeful rest.

2ND CITIZEN: Aye, brother; but for these holidays when we forget out daily work we would become simply mechanical, forget all day long of fire and hammers and bellows, or awls and leather and old shoes, of high prices and low earnings. What is worse, these accursed thoughts chase us even in our dreams, as though to mind us even then of our eternal trades.

1ST CITIZEN: Whilst in holidays one passes a pleasant day with his friends and family, conversing and jesting on idle matters leisurely, fondling the while one's children; and in the afternoon, after a warm dinner of meats and soup stroll lazily without the city-gates amidst the scenes of Nature till the sun

Valentio Di'Buondelmonte

sinks low, or betake oneself to a tavern to empty a few cups of good old sack.

2ND CITIZEN: But poor devils, we are compelled by fear of starvation to sweat even on God's day, as though He made that day only for those knights who loiter about the streets the livelong day, to cure their boredom by brawls and thrusts, or drowsy in noisy banquets and endless revelry in all manner of excessive drink and heavy foods like swine, blissfully ignorant of the thorns of life. [*Enter* 3RD CITIZEN]

3RD CITIZEN: Good morrow, brethren.

1ST *and* 2nd citizens [*together*]: Good morrow, brother.

3RD CITIZEN: Will you not to church this morn?

1ST CITIZEN: Yea, by and by.

2ND CITIZEN: The day is young yet. *Enter conspirators at back of stage*

1ST CITIZEN: These look not like holiday-makers. They seem bent on unholy deeds.

2ND CITIZEN: They rejoice in the Lord's rising with instruments of war, methinks!

3RD CITIZEN: God protect us from the wiles of the devil!

1ST *and* 2nd citizens [*together*]: Amen! [*Distant sound of church-bells is heard*]

[*Together*] Christ hath risen from the dead!

3RD CITIZEN: Come, brethren, let us away; the bells call us to holy mass. [*Exeunt* CITIZENS]

[*Conspirators come to front part of stage conversing in low tones*]

ODDO [*says something to* BERNARDO *in a low voice.* BERNARDO *shakes his head knowingly*]

ACT IV

BERNARDO:
> Beatrice. . . . It minds me of her flight!
> Who would have guessed that she could be restored
> In such quick wise!

FRANCESCO:
> Fair chance did smile to them
> When they did meet that pilgrim without
> The city-gates: was it not he that spake
> To them what made them know it was to Rome
> These lovers aimed? This pilgrim must needs have
> Keen eyes to note them in the early morn.

ODDO:
> Pilgrims have keener eyes than their vocation
> Doth demand, meseems.

LORENZO:
> No matter. Had
> They parted company ere they had seen
> The pilgrim, the knowledge gained might well have served
> Them not: one might not have been the equal
> Of such a desperate lover!

FRANCESCO:
> True.

ODDO:
> But I deem it unwise of them when once
> They had compelled him to yield
> His most unlawful prize, to have him spared.
> They should have eased him of his freedom.
> For I've misgivings that he will be fool
> Enough to cherish in his heart the thought
> Of high success through a second attempt
> Where once he failed. Now that the fault is done
> And may not be undone, we needs must keep
> Strict watch to foil such an attempt.

Valentio Di'Buondelmonte

LORENZO [*impatiently*]:
> Let the
> Dead past flatter himself with what attention
> We're rendered him: the present is our interest. [*to* ODDO]
> Hast thou a strong assurance that may ease
> The doubts within my sceptic heart? It tells
> Me that Valentio will not pass this way
> Today: thou knowest, the heart is of prophetic.

FRANCESCO:
> Then wilt thou us to heed such an uncertain
> Guide, and with an old dame's credulence
> Let this day wane, this morn that we've
> Awaited with a miser's strict account,
> To attend again upon some another
> Opportunity to execute our intent?

ODDO [*to* LORENZO]:
> There is no greater knave or liar
> Than the heart. 'Tis ever there to lead
> Our wandering steps astray and make of us
> Our own poor fools; ourselves our laughing-stocks;
> At once the actors and the audience.
> What makes Valentio go to his swift doom
> If not his heart? I trow he'd rather
> Lose life itself than not behold his Love
> This Easter morn. I know these lovers well,
> My friend, trust not like them, thy heart.

BERNARDO:
> What if
> He doth suspect an ambush? He cannot
> Be as thoughtless as not to know that we
> Will not abide in slavish fashion his
> Outrageous perjury.

ACT IV

Oddo:
> Thou creditest him
> With more forethought than thou needst. Bah! He who
> Allow his heart be conquered by the frail
> Storming of feminine art cannot be
> Too careful. Nay, not Valentio!
> Let us therefore be in readiness
> That when he comes he may dispatched be
> The quickest. [*Utters a short, dry laugh*] Be quick to action when
> You see him. Tarry not till he handles
> His sword, or else he will cause us a Hell
> Of trouble; yea, he by himself, with the four
> Of us. He's no mean wielder of the sword,
> By the Devil! [*aside*] But soft, were they my lips
> That uttered "Dispatched quickly"? ... [*aloud*] And yet
> Is not the heart that fain would have
> The brief moments of his mortal agony
> Expand and so extend so as to fill
> The whole expanse of Time to its utmost Poles?
> Nay more; that in these sweetest moments, Time,
> That hare-foot runner light may pause in
> His endless track to gather breath; so might
> My joy proportionate be? But here's the worst
> Portion of all. For I must lie content
> With but his death, which may (who knows)
> But be the very best of goods! For may
> Not death, which we all dread, be but the path
> To greater joys to the living denied?
> What irony, what playful irony
> In Fate's most solemn act!

[*Enter* Valentio *gaily "attired in a vest of fine woollen cloth, a white mantle thrown across his shoulders and the wedding garland on his head." As soon as he reaches the "time-worn" statute of the Roman god Mars, which dominates the plaza, the conspirators attack him*]

Valentio Di'Buondelmonte

VALENTIO [*trying to snatch out his sword*]:

Ha! Trying
Your skill on Easter morn?!
[*With his mace* SCHIATTI *fells him to the ground, and at the base of this grim idol the daggers of* ODDO *and his furious kinsmen finish the savage deed*]
Oh, you cowards! [*Dies, with the bridal wreath "dangling from his brow a bloody and ill-omened sacrifice"*]

ODDO [*aside*]:

Rejoice, my soul, and O my eyes, drink deep
Of vengeance's richest beams! Drink till
Satiety bid thee to pause, not less;
For verily such sweetness makes of gall
The nectar which the gods on high Olympus
Sip, and causes Love (which fools deem sweet)
To blush with crimson shame! Such is this joy
Which simpletons can never know! [*aloud*] Go
Merry yourselves for this occasion; revel;
Be generous with wine! I've drunk my part. [*Points to the corpse*]
[*Exeunt Conspirators*]
[*Enter* LIVIA *and* STEFANO. *They are not aware of the body*]

STEFANO:

Wherefore does my lady tax her tender body by walking such a long distance? If you will allow I'll proceed alone and bring you the news quickly.

LIVIA:

If love bids me go to the frozen Pole
I would obey!

STEFANO:

Be it as you will, my lady; though still methinks, since you have waited much ere this day, your patience may endure a little more.

ACT IV

LIVIA:
>Not so, Stefano: My heart can keep no more within its bounds
>The love that hath welled up with great
>Travail, as of childbirth since I beheld
>Him last: this pain augments if it be not
>on him bestowed.
>[STEFANO *looks around him accidentally and sees the body. He turns pale and is unable to reply.* LIVIA *notices that something went wrong*]
>Why gazest thou at me
>With such distracted eyes?

STEFANO [*with difficulty*]:
>'Tis nothing worthy of your attention: just a pain that sometimes
>visits me
>and then as suddenly forsakes me. But I beseech you my lady,
>to heed my past words.

LIVIA:
>Nay, thou shalt go home: Thou seem'st
>To be sick. I'll go alone.
>[*She turns to continue her way and catches sight of* VALENTIO'S *body, utters a stifled cry and is about to faint.* STEFANO *supports her.*]
>[*Pathetically:*]
>Tell me
>It is not true; that my love lives yet.
>O speak! . . . [STEFANO *remains silent*] *Then, in a parched voice*:

STEFANO:
>Let us flee this fiendish place. [*Tries to make her move*]

LIVIA:
>O no, divide me not from him! [*Falls on the body. Faintly:*]
>Speak to me my love; speak, I've come, thy Love,

Valentio Di'Buondelmonte

Thy Livia ... wouldst thou keep silent thus
Forever. . . . ? [*Her tears fall silently, mingling with his blood.
Puts her hand on his brow*]
Ah me! Death's frosty dew hath chilled Thy blanched brow
... [*Sees the deep gashes from which blood continues to well*]
Thy precious life
Is ebbing with thy precious gore, and mine
Also is ebbing with it. . . . Will no one
Stop these dark gashes, yawning abysses
Reaching to thy heart, through which Death unveils
Himself, from pouring blood and more blood?! ...
Ah me, that this thy heart, the sacred shrine
Of Love should thus be trampled
Under the feet ... !
[*Enter* UBERTO, *deep in thought*]

UBERTO:

Fool! Unhappy fool! To let
These hirelings chill my resistance by
The force of number, nothing more! They should
Have forced my breath away ere force my heart
To yield his love! What cruel mercy,
Not to bereave me of my life, as though death
Was not sufficient punishment for loving!
But they know not that they had already
Bereft me of more than life's self, and so
Could die no more. They've left this shadow
To roam beneath these imprisoning battlements
As though its sphere, not as of your rapturous
Thrill like as the quiver of the leaves
In the soft wind, or like the heaving of
The lyre beneath the frenzied fingers of
The bard, but with a mad tempest of woe
And with a heavy heart, made heavier
By the remembrance of happiness lost,
Bitter for sweetness flown; with painful
Consolation that in this dungeon of

ACT IV

The body a heart is free in loving yet.
[*lifts his eyes and sees* VALENTIO's *body, but does not recognize it because Livia hangs on it like a drooping lily. Exclaims:*]
Ha! What do mine eyes behold: a Graveyard,
A battlefield, the day of Doom? Is this
God's swift courier bent o'er this mortal clod
To lift the e'er enduring soul to His
Empyrean Throne? [*Approaches it and recognizes* VALENTIO's *body*]
Eyes start from your orbs;
Let mine revolting hair stand on an end,
And thou O furious heart batter my breast
O'er this foul earth! Alack, alack, my friend,
Valentio, drowned in thy own priceless gore.
Oh, thou that were wont to bathe in the moon's
Golden beams! For thee no more the boughs
Shall dance in glee; the nested bird repeat
Thy cherished song, and thrill at his own sweet
Voice, and the morning breeze steal a kiss
From thy wanton hair, and wrapt with wonder and
Delight to linger there, forgetful of
The theft. The Harvester's blind scythe hath felled
Thy tender buds whilst yet half-oped to life's
New-wakened Sun, and left, alack, the thorns,
Rude thorns, and briers harsh . . . .
[*Sees the wedding garland that lay stained with blood, and the wedding ring*]
Ah me, thou hast
Indeed been wed to Death, the cold-eyed Maid;
And this: [*Pointing to the garland*] forsooth's thy wedding wreathe!
Ah wherefore fallen in eternal Sleep?
What heart would smile to see thee fallen?
[*Slowly*] He was to wed Beatrice; where was she then,
Aye, where was she? . . . [*Suddenly bursts out:*]
Ah, a scapegoat, made
To bear the wrath of Di'Ameidei for

Valentio Di'Buondelmonte

Her flight. It would indeed rejoice Oddo.
Yea, killed before the Castle! Ah me,
Wherefore did I not warn him to beware
A danger perchance creeping in the Night? But oh,
It asks divining eyes to see that Woe
Would thus be born of Bliss. Beside, could I
Unveil to him my secret purposes? Again,
What boot? For he is bold and fearless as
The lion of the forest, and would laugh
That death hath fixed his unerring shaft
To murder him. Alack, his boldness
Was his undoing. [*Observes* Livia *weeping in silence. To he*r:]
Woman, who art thou,
Disturbing him in his repose? Thou dost
Not mourn a knight by wetting his cold corpse
With tears, but by bathing him in his murderer's
Blood! If he be dear to thee, let the
Fount of thy tears in thy bosom be dried
By the fierce flame of hate, and the fire
Of form resolve to avenge his outrageous death
Flash in thy eyes! No tears, but crimson blood
Freely flowing; and by this grim idol
Of fire and fury. [*Points to the statue of Mars*]
He shall have it!
[*Bends over the body*]
Sleep thou in peace. This firm arm thou
Didst rescue from the chill of death shall be
To thee e'en as a second arm to fell
Thy enemies!
[*Beckons to* Stefano. *They carry the body away while* Livia *is still bent over her husband's pallid features*]
[*Re-enter simultaneously from opposite sides:* Uberto, *sword in hand, and Conspirators*]
I had not thought that villains
Dare cross the damned site that witnessed
Their dark unholy deeds, where every stone
Is a keen eye, and every pebble

ACT IV

A mouth to betray the murderer: thou should'st
Bury your faces in dark corners, far
From human paths, lest swift Justice o'ertake
You whilst your hands are dyed with gore, and read
Your crimes, written in bloody characters in
Your fearful eyes.

ODDO:

Zounds! Thou pinest
To join thy friend in Hell that thou dost dare
To cross my way.

UBERTO:

Thou speakest of fighting!?

ODDO:

Beware, rash youth; go if thou pitiest thee
And break thy sword; or else, by all the fiends,
Thou shalt soon die a mad dog's death!

UBERTO:

I'd rather
Break my sword on thy back if thou wert not
Worthy only of being beaten with
A cudgel! Come, quick (if thou beest he
Who struck him down), and face my sword.

BERNARDO:

I can
No more list to this lunatic's babble:
I'll silence him.

ODDO:

No, wait. Let him relieve
His mind before he dies: 'twill serve for a
Confession.

Valentio Di'Buondelmonte

UBERTO:
> Nay, confess thy sins first,
> For thou shalt die ere these cowards do stab
> Me from my back: take heed. [*Attacks him. They fight.*
> ODDO *is wounded*]

ODDO:
> The knave!
> He's killing me!
> [*The others attack* UBERTO *and overcome his stout resistance, mortally wounding him*]

UBERTO [*Dying*]:
> Valentio, . . . Forgive me Beatrice. . . . [*Dies*]
> [*Exeunt conspirators, supporting* ODDO]

ACT V

Scene: A room in Lambertuccio's Castle

[*Enter* BEATRICE, *as though talking to herself*]

BEATRICE:
    How changed, my God how changed, and in such
    A brief span! Scarce seems he himself, grown old
    In days what others grow in years. Deeply
    Are traced by sorrow's finger rude the lines
    Of pain upon his brow, and woe's dark mist
    Hangs darkly in his spark-less eyes.
    The smile still hovers o'er his convulsed lips,
    Perchance unconscious of his plight, or as
    A painted mask to put off curious eyes
    From secret scrutiny, and so unveil
    Tyrant Despair, pensive, in his heart's core,
    Enthroned there with ball and sceptre meet,
    Unrivaled lord of his precious demesne;
    Yea, waxing rich on poverty, fattened
    On famine. O how difficult, my God
    How difficult to be compelled to play
    The jester's fun or the merry actor's farce
    Before the blind, contented audience,
    Whilst the real veiled self behind the stage
    Is hourly stabbed with viewless knives in his

Valentio Di'Buondelmonte

Unattended Tragedy with every jest
The actor makes; and when the alien others
Depart, and the actor doth quit the stage,
Empties his flowing woe on his un-consoled
Pillow, and shakes the solid walls with groans
And sighs: to be two selves and seem but one;
Himself be not himself: alien unto it.
For I have felt full sore O my father
Since that most sweetest day and bitterest,
In every look and word of thine that thou
Offerest thy love as ever where thou
Expectest to receive no more; a lonely,
A hopeless love: love in despair; a somber
Light; a shadowed brightness; night in day,
And this, alas, is woe's sharpest pang:
If, like a swift meteor this love, with its
Own flame itself consumed, or else if thou
Didst but expel it from thy heart's Eden,
As came to pass with our First Parents Old,
Then it were easier far. It had caused me
Less pain, forsooth. But wait! Is not
Love perfect in itself, unto itself
Sufficient? With itself content?
A universe of its own?—What, deceive
Myself with these smooth words? Yet why? for I
Love him: who durst say I love him not!
I love him since I learnt that which love is,
When clad in naked majesty, revealed
Himself, as God to Moses in Sinai.
'Tis strange indeed to grieve that I have loved:
Could I love him, not knowing love? Doth Love
Bid us to love and yet not love? Embrace Him
By drawing away from His extended arms?
To love without loving? Love envieth
Love? Is it not One, Undivided? Oh
Were that all! I have learnt
The loss of Love: Uberto, chiefest of

ACT V

My woes; theme of my bitterest tears. 'Tis not
That thou art dead; for Love is life, and Death
Is not where Life is: there is no Love
And Death. Death's powerless to divide what Love
Hath joined; and I could fly so easily
The dark dungeon of Life if Death were but the only
Prison-gate betwixt us; but thou hast
Forsaken me by thy very death. 'Tis plain
That failure dire hath dragged love's radiant star,
That scattered its joy-laden beams, outshining
The Evening Star, like to a falling meteor,
Adown the abyss of despair and quenched
It there; thus purposeless in Life's myriad ways,
No more a pilgrim to Love's distant shrine,
Didst stake thy precious life for a low gain;
Prodigal in thy most precious possession,
Disposing it as though it were thine own
Alone, not mine also: nay, mine far more.
Revenge! What mockery! Love a beggar
At Friendship's door, entreating to be heard
In vain; nay, driven off like to a dog
By proud Oblivion! A paramour
Into whose credulous ears is poured the dew of
Endearments sweet, yet soon to be forgot
When on another maid displays her charms
More gaudy, dexterously arrayed, before
The raptured eye! What truth reviled,
Order made Chaos, Reality unreal,
Subject made lord and Lord with menials placed!
For lo! Love, Lord of the Soul, before
Whose sovereignty Friendship should bend the knee
Of homage meek, hath risen in rash rebellion,
His throne usurping, claiming obedience low
Of him who knows how to receive, but not
To give, indeed avenge, a friend! I must
Ne'er harbour in my breast the hope of Death:
Death serves me not; it is a Night that hath

Valentio Di'Buondelmonte

A Morn—Love's Death is an eternal Sleep,
Unbroke e'en by the Dreams of Happiness past;
A Death without Resurrection. To wake
From death waketh me not from Death! I
Must turn my face towards warm life; I must love
Live! Live! By very life I shall
Forsake *him* as he hath forsaken me [*starts as from sleep*]
Live! Did I say "Live"! O Hell! Live, when
Life's sap is dried? Damnation! I love
Him yet! Infernal powers! I love him yet!
Love is invincible! [*pulls a dagger from her bosom*]
[*to the dagger*: Let thy cold steel
Destroy what love hath built. Let naught remain
To tell that Love had once dwelt there! [*Stabs herself in the breast*] Oh . . . [*Dies*]
[*Enter* Livia]

Livia [*With an expressionless face slowly goes towards the body*]
I had not thought death so simple, so sure
In its embrace, so swift in its cure!
But one brief moment, and all is over . . .
[*Bends over* Beatrice's *body and pulls the dagger dripping with blood from her breast; gazes at the dagger for a few moments, then brings it to her breast. Frightened:*] No! I dare not!
[*Throws the dagger down, shuddering*]
The path of Death is lonely
And dark, with what horrid dangers perchance
Beset? What hideous monsters, what abysses
Gaping wide, that made the blood to freeze
And to obstruct its channels to the heart
No mortal thought may fathom, no fancy
Paint. Ah me, to sail alone on that
Wide and dark sea, a creature frail as I,
With no beacon or pilot-star to steer
My course to the farther shore: Prayer and Faith
No use have they to me; rather they'll be
A warning and a threat, eternal curse,

ACT V

God's preordained sentence just to those
Rebellious spirits that with insolence proud
And most impious hands reject and stain
God's vested garment. Hell, where Love and Peace
Dwell not but writhing pain and wailing, midst
The most abhorred of men; and there how shall
I stand before God's throne to claim my Love?
Alas, if Hell itself could us unite
I'd do it. [*pauses*] Then since the Gates of Death
Are barred for me, I'll to a convent
Where the iron bars and the sacred garb
Doubly imprisoning my ancient self
Will make me free, like as a one newly
Born from the womb, to build a newer life
Upon the ruins of the old: there will
I pray and fast, and all the sacred rites
Observe, to bring God's balm to bruised souls,
Though none to me, like to a sage well read
In Galen's art that can administer not
To his own ailments; for I know full well
How vain it is to flee from a living self
(Though fettered), which will haunt my prayers
And loneliness, and silent nights, and all
My ancient life will rise as from the tomb
With all life's pulse, and then, fleeing
Will there be none. Oh, forgive me Love,
Flee from my sweetest memories, from Life
In Death! They shall become the bond betwixt
My love and me, until the day of Union
Dawns, ah, when it dawns.... [*Her eyes are filled with tears. From outside the sound of swords and steel, mixed with shouts, is heard:*]
Hack! Burn!
Death to the Donati! Death to the Buondelmontii!
To the Castle! Hang the old hag! Hang the old witch!
Oh God! Livia [*casts one last look at* BEATRICE's *body, then exits hurriedly*]

Part Two

Valentio Di' Buondelmonte

A Verse Tragedy in Five Acts

New Version (2012)

ACT I

Scene: A Public Square in Florence

[*Enter three* CITIZENS]

1ST CITIZEN [*to* 2ND CITIZEN, *who is silent*]: Now, now, why are you silent? What disturbing thoughts have robbed you of speech?

2ND CITIZEN: No, fears that lie deeper than the sounding of words.

1ST CITIZEN: Come man; surely you do not mean one of those petty fears which ever dye your cheeks with a sickly hue!

2ND CITIZEN: I heartily wish it were so. But wait; has not reached your ears what happened a few days past? It is now the general talk of Florence.

3RD CITIZEN: Do you mean the broil between the Ameidei and Uberto and his friend Valentio?

2ND CITIZEN: No other.

1ST CITIZEN: Well, well; broils, what else? It sounds new to my ears.

2ND CITIZEN: Lend them to me, then, and I'll repeat to you what imperfect knowledge has been carried to mine by the

Valentio Di'Buondelmonte

winds of rumor: For reasons not known through some allege it to be no more than the heat of the occasion which, I think, must have been deeply rooted in his heart, nourished by passing time: a concealed hate that clad in words gave vent to itself, Oddo (a very fiery and bold youth) flung hot insults in Uberto's furious face in the midst of a banquet gathering the Flower of the town, whilst in noisy merriment and lavish feasting, where the gilded cups were never emptied of golden wine. . . . Uberto, impatient of the insult, did not restrain his wounded pride from answering back in sharpest terms; whereupon Oddo, replying with his sword assailed the unexpecting youth, and would surely have slain him, had not Valentio, with friendly rage, and with eager arm forced Oddo's sword to miss its mark; nay, more, he carved a deep gash in Oddo's frame, and would have added more had he not deemed it answer enough to Oddo's arrogance. Thereupon, the banquet was drawn into two and a general fight might have concluded, and God knows what noble blood might have flowed that day, had not some more sober among them scattered the aroused parties. I know no more. But my scarce knowledge is a rich foreboding of a tempest drawing near which will hurl its thunderbolts on our reposing town and burn it with Hellish fire.

3RD CITIZEN: Your fears are no baseless fancy-fabric. Foul rumors (more foul than their begetters) infest the startled air: Oddo's kin, it is claimed, declining bloodless terms, are banding themselves and drawing to them their scattered forces, and many a friendly house in Florence looks with favoring eyes on these matters.

1ST CITIZEN: It is hard indeed for my credulence to grant this strange news; my fancy revolts to figure these peaceful streets made a bloody battlefield.

2ND CITIZEN: Amen! [*to* 3RD CITIZEN] And in what manner has the Duke welcomed the news?

ACT I

3RD CITIZEN: It is not yet known. But he's our only hope. Let's pray that he will prevent this woe, that these foul rumors may seem the idle inventions of overwrought brains, with no more substance of truth than a dream.

[*They exit. Enter* ODDO, LAMBERTUCCIO, *and* RINIERI]

LAMB. [*to* ODDO]:
About your new broil; adding one more to the
quick-swelling number of your foolish deeds
I'm well informed; echoed by Florence. What's
graver still is you planning bitter bloody strife
and would not espouse fair peace.

ODDO:
Fair peace! Fair indeed, if wedded to downcast-eyed
disgrace! Your words fall on my startled ear
like sounds from some strange land: that you should
know, being of D'Ameidei's blood as I; but its
not strange to you since your lips are guilty.
Peace! How dearly bought when purchased with
the coins of shame!

RINIERI:
There's no disgrace, since it does not dwell with valor,
whose right arm you are; rather, it will be made known
that it is but through disdain to strike and not through fear
that you do not return Valentio's blows with blows [*after a pause:*]
though even if you did truly fear to rouse his kind, whose name
makes half of Florence tremble, your valor's sheen would not
be dulled.

LAMB.:
Most wisely said; and yet you wrong us by doubt;
were our cause just, nothing could make us
decline the field though all the powers of Hell

Valentio Di'Buondelmonte

    were to oppose us. But with Valentio justice lies,
    and to him Justice shall be done. Then
    is not Peace the least we can offer?

Oddo:

    Do not name again that hateful word that falls
    like the screech of night's foul bird on my enraged ears
    making my blood boil in my throbbing veins.

Lamb.:

    Your words are untamed by sober thought;
    will you then have Florence aflame with war?
    you can't be ignorant how it unloosens
    chained evil's might, marring the beauty
    of the world with blood and fire; making
    it a Hell where it should be a human Paradise—
    and shall we fight between ourselves and let
    the envious foes of happy Florence be merry
    at her woe? This incident is of little consequence:
    leave it to time, it will heal both wounds alike.

Oddo:

    Bid me forget all things dear to my heart,
    and all the joys of life—even life itself,
    and lie in a cold tomb and rot; but not
    the bold outrage that left the eloquent mark
    of its mockery on my revolting frame
    an everlasting stain, exposed to scorn, traced
    by pointing fingers, which when do not point
    eyes cry: "Behold the white-cheeked coward"!

Rinieri [*aside, reflecting on* Oddo's *last words*]:

    Poor honor, how I pity you, since you have
    nothing but wavering opinion to nourish you,
    swayed by the caprice of mere men, and by
    every blast of various thought; yes, you're
    miserable. I would not have you in my company. [*to* Lamb.
    and Oddo:]

ACT I

Let's go to the Duke, since you're at variance with me,
whose sound and noble mind has earned him fame
like Israel's old sceptered sage; for there, Justice
his mild domain unfurls. . . .

ODDO [*aside*]:

. . . to that old fool! [*in a loud voice:*]
Yes, to demand justice, denied me here.
But if I don't find it I'll seek it elsewhere.
[*All except* ODDO *exit.* ODDO *mutters between his teeth*:] You
shall not escape me, for all their words! [*Exits*]

[*Enter* DUKE *of Florence, attended by his retinue,* FLOURISH]

DUKE [*talking to himself*]:

Most unhappy Florence! How soon the somber shadows
of dire destruction threaten to fall again on your life's sunny
way and bleach the rosy cheeks with pallid fear, repeating
for the hundredth time the sorry tale in its bloody history—
Sodom doomed to be dyed forever with gore;
your silent streets forever haunted by the specter of death,
and your great palaces the banquet-halls of reveling Mars!—
for these haughty slaves whose hearts rejoice in civil blood
rather than to unsheathe their eager swords in the stern faces
of Florence's common foes; while I am doomed
to play a poor spectator's sorry part, possessing not the power
to do anything else, compelled to taste the bitterness to be
in name the ruler, in power not. But could I force the fleeting
years to retrace their dusty steps, regain the unflinching,
stout heart of youth, pour warm ardor and Herculean zeal
to my sore trembling arms, I would not linger here uttering
vain words. O idle wish bred of impotence! –what redress
remains save to try to reconcile the alienated hearts?

[*Re-enter* ODDO, LAMB., VALENTIO, *and* RINIERI]

ODDO [*addressing the* DUKE]:

My Lord, I come demanding that Justice be done to me.

Valentio Di'Buondelmonte

DUKE:
> Have you been wronged?

ODDO:
> Yes, wronged, abused, scorned in the midst of gentlemen, made a justice-seeking fool, while the root and cause of all is free like a soaring, sharp-beaked eagle, perhaps for my undoing.

DUKE:
> You awaken my curiosity to learn the name of the bold offender:
> Pray tell me who?

ODDO:
> A name my furious lips would scorch if they try to spell it. It's not a stranger to your ears.

RINIERI:
> It spells 'Valentio,' Your Highness. [*Enter Valentio and Uberto*]

DUKE:
> Ah, here he comes. [*to* VALENTIO] This gentleman [*points to* ODDO] claims amends for certain wrongs he maintains you've done him.
> How would you defend yourself against the charge?

VALENTIO [*after a pause*]:
> Both my silence and his wound plead him right.

UBERTO:
> Not so, my Lord. It's I, not he, who should suffer your wrath.

VALENTIO:
> No, don't heed him, my Lord. He speaks this way driven by a generous nature.

ACT I

DUKE [*to* VALENTIO *and* UBERTO]:

> I truly marvel at your words. I haven't seen before this day
> men so much in love with punishment! I commend
> your noble friendship yet demand to know who the offender
> is.

VALENTIO:

> It's I.

UBERTO:

> No, it's I.

DUKE [*reflecting*]:

> Since each of you so firmly wants to bear the charge and
> is unshaken in his judgment, it seems to me well to devise
> some other way to extricate us from this difficulty. [*to Lamb.*]
> you have a beautiful daughter, a maiden more fair but no less
> bright
> than heaven's sun, whom I beheld one day happier than any in
> my life.
> So surpassing fair was she that amorous Time, wounded by
> the darts of Love, fled with haste lest he be wounded more
> I did not know how. She made me rue my palsied age
> and envy most bold youth.

LAMB. [*bowing low*]:

> My Lord, you flood my humble self with all this generous
> praise,
> beyond all hope of thanks I abide in debt.

DUKE:

> She's called Beatrice, is she not?

UBERTO [*aside, with his hand on his heart*]:

> Hush, fond heart, you make me believe it was her name I
> heard!

Valentio Di'Buondelmonte

ODDO [*aside, impatiently*]:
> The devil, the Duke turned out a doting lover!

DUKE:
> Most becoming name for one who has eyes
> that make the jealous Queen of Night
> quit in shame, and heaven's lights burn out
> themselves with spite.

UBERTO [*aside*]:
> Of her he must be speaking, since to whom other than her
> can this description fit?
> and yet I fear my ears play me false, or I wake
> in an idle dream with semblance of reality.

DUKE:
> She's a virgin rose newly blown from the bud, thus fitting
> that amorous butterflies should woo her
> from her maiden dreams.

LAMB.:
> Do you mean, My Lord, that she should marry?

DUKE:
> Yes; that I meant.

UBERTO [*aside*]:
> O joy! What a glorious hope swells from the dark deeps
> of my heart, like the glorious break of day
> after a weary night. Yet I dare not cherish it
> for long and feed it with my slumbering dreams
> lest its life-span be brief even as it is glorious.

LAMB.:
> To whom, My Lord?

DUKE:
> Why, to Valentio: and the gall of hatred, like
> a summer cloud will pass away

ACT I

ODDO [*aside, angrily*]:
    By the Devil! A lunatic would not utter such a
    damned outrage. [*aloud*] My Lord, surely
    you're only jesting, though I must confess
    it does not amuse me.

UBERTO [*aside*]:
    Great heavens! Have you heard all this? No, No,
    it cannot be! What man would steal my Love
    from me—not my friend! My wrought
    imagination is fooling me. Yes, it's my imagination! [*tries to
    laugh, but it is hollow and he starts*]
    Why does my laugh sound so, and why did I start?

DUKE [*to* ODDO]:
    Why do you marvel. It's very simple. [*to* VALENTIO] What do
    you say?

VALENTIO:
    My thanks to Your Highness for your most generous offer.
    But whether I do espouse a fair maiden or colder
    Fate, it's one to me. No, if any of the gentlemen
    for whatever reason, thinks the contrary
    of what Your Highness proposes, it's my desire
    to bear Your wrath and punishment
    than be mistook for some wife-sheltered coward.

DUKE [*turning to* LAMB. *and* ODDO]:
    What say you?

LAMB.:
    I'm of your mind, Your Highness.

ODDO:
    I'm not—you're murdering justice!

LAMB.:
    No. It's my private right to grant consent
    or to refrain. [*to* RINIERI] what do you think?

Valentio Di'Buondelmonte

RINIERI:
> It's proper that he marry your daughter. [*in an undertone*] He seems a worthy gentleman.

VALENTIO:
> My Lord, I . . . .

DUKE [*interrupting him*]:
> No more protests!

ODDO:
> You band yourselves against me. I shall stand it no more! [*Aside, looking at* VALENTIO *with flaming eyes and clenched fist*]
> You have again escaped me—and with a beautiful bride! Blessed sleep, visit no more those burning eyes; and light-hearted ease, forsake my breast till I drink the sweet wine of revenge to the last dregs. *Exits*

DUKE [*to* VALENTIO, *who is pensive*]:
> Why, you look like a lover hopeless in love. A clouded brow befits no bridegroom: certainly not for such a bride!

RINIERI:
> He marvels at his good fortune, I think.

DUKE:
> Yes, that he should, in due order; but [*turning to* LAMB.] first appoint a day to pledge his troth.

LAMB.:
> Presently Your Highness. [*going*]

RINIERI [*whispering in* LAMB.*'s ear*]:
> I told you, the Duke is wise! *All exit*

Act II

Scene: A Room in Lambertuccio's Castle

As the curtain rises Beatrice is discovered pacing the room excitedly

BEATRICE:
    The sands have all run out, and he still tarries …
    what can make him so late? I fear some mishap
    has befallen him.
    [*She stops suddenly and listens*]
    Can it be his footsteps?
    [*Finding that there is no sound*]
    Troubled minds thwart the natural offices of Nature…
    [*She continues to pace the room*]
    What if he does not come?
    [*Several taps are heard. She rushes to the door and opens it*]
    It's he at last!

UBERTO [*still outside, cautiously protrudes his head inside*]:
    Are you alone?

BEATRICE:
    Yes, have no fears. Father's out and the maid's
    on an errand. [UBERTO *enters*]
    My Love, how cruel you are to tarry so long!

Valentio Di'Buondelmonte

    I thought lovers have more gentle hearts. But no,
the fire of love in your breast must have
expired; else how could you buy anything
with the dear price of love's joy?

UBERTO:

    Let the warmth of my kisses prove
that it has waxed stronger;
or if you but put your hand to my heart
and feel how it throbs for you. But No!
It's fire would surely scorch your hand
this is why love has led me here: to lull it
into the lap of sleep with your soft looks;
though soon, alas, to wake up again
with greater might, since the cause of my ailment
is my cure; like that bronze serpent that God's
Chosen People erected in the sandy ocean. [*kisses her*]

BEATRICE:

    If this kiss could live forever, that I may cling
to it and thus remain in changeless bliss amid
capricious Fate's eternal inconstancy! Or gazing
into the love-lit depths of your dark eyes, to plunge
in their infinitude until the very abode
of your chaste soul, and with it mingle,
and so forget, as in Lethe's silent stream
fears more dark than silent nights, conjured
before my eyes in all horrid shapes—for did
we not live those holy moments stolen
from the angels? Not many may attain more.
Then what remains to us but death
to free them from Fate's icy eternal grip:
the everlasting refuge from dire decline and suffering,
if not estrangement?

UBERTO:

    Dear Love, what wayward thoughts have slid

Act II

into your beautiful little head! How can
light and darkness dwell together in your heart?
Your fears are fancy-woven; and what
reward have we to strain our weakling eyes in vain
attempts to pierce the mist of tomorrow? Let us
enjoy the heaven-sent bliss before it's too late.

BEATRICE:

It's only wise to fear the tempest when the sea
seems most calm. Why does Heaven reserve
the bitterest cup to lovers?!

UBERTO:

To put to proof their constancy; which if they bear
with constant minds and changeless passion
it grants them eternal bliss in un-severable
unity, though sometimes after they cast off
their earthly raiment; and besides, dear lady,
only great pain brings forth great happiness:
they go together, hand in hand. For are not
roses by their thorns made fair?

BEATRICE [*noticing that he is paler than usual*]:

I think the thorns of love have started to pierce your heart—
or why have you grown more pale?

UBERTO:

My paleness is but the reflection of your fears...
[*Footsteps are heard outside*]

BETRICE [*agitated*]:

My father! Hide behind the curtain!

UBERTO:

No, let me hide where I may still feast
my famished eyes on you loveliness.
I cannot endure losing sight of you.

83

Valentio Di'Buondelmonte

BEATRICE:
> Quick, no more! [UBERTO *hides*. Enter LAMB.]

LAMB.:
> I bring you joyful news, daughter, that will revive
> (I hope) your drooping and withering petals,
> which less-knowing men would charge to love's
> intemperate beams. But I well know you're wise
> and would not expose yourself to them
> like foolish youth that languishes for love.

BEATRICE:
> It's well and good if it can work such magic.

LAMB.:
> You are versed (in no way worse than
> many a cloistered nun) in the Holy Scripture;
> how Man and Woman were created
> twin trees with boughs entwined,
> growing on the same soil, warmed by
> the very-same sun, by the same breezes caressed.

BEATRICE [*impatiently*]:
> Indeed! And yet I do not see the good news in this…

LAMB.:
> Patience, daughter! Let me proceed. Since you are
> a child no more, it behooves you to wed a gentleman
> of culture and gentle breed. You're most fortunate
> that such a winsome and handsome gentleman
> has asked your hand, and wishes to make you
> his bride within two days.

BEATRICE:
> I myself have long ordained a Bride to Christ
> within Santa Maggiore's quiet walls, not to a mortal man.

Act II

LAMB.:
> You've drawn little from your life's store, and so
> it's unwise to lavish the future's richer treasure,
> which those whose store has always run out
> can do without loss. No, it's even a crime
> to cut off the warm sap of human joys
> from your young and supple stem and cause
> your new-blown blossoms of most lovely hue,
> which should delight a dainty eye,
> to wither before they bear fruit.

BEATRICE:
> But father...

LAMB. [*stopping her with a motion of his hand*]:

BEATRICE:
> Suffer me to speak...

LAMB.:
> Enough! [*aside*]
> I should know women better. Its maiden coyness
> that makes her speak this way, and perhaps
> a little of feminine art. [*aloud*] Tomasso, Tomasso!
> [*Enter* TOMASSO]

TOMASSO:
> Your pleasure, Sir?

LAMB.:
> Show your skill, man, and deck the table
> with delicious dishes that will invite
> a lusty appetite. [TOMASSO *bows and is leaving*]
> And, do not forget the sparkling wine. [TOMASSO *exits*]
> [*to* BEATRICE]
> Your future husband and some
> of our old friends are coming;
> therefore prepare yourself to meet them;

Valentio Di'Buondelmonte

and remember your wedding. [LAMB. *exits*]

BEATRICE:

Woe without number or end . . . [UBERTO *comes out of hiding*]
Did you hear?

UBERTO:

Alas, if hearing were all! Say rather: "Did you feel it? Did
the accents rush upon your wounded ear with all the loosened
might of thunder, shaking your inmost nerves and fibers,
working havoc with your soul as armed with lightning's
electric might? Did the ground tremble under your feet
as if to gape and hide you in its earthy bowels
from the woe to come? And yet, alas! This all was only
the augmentation of the bleeding of a wounded heart,
since I carried the heavy burden of knowledge all the time.

BEATRICE [*talks to herself in a loud voice*]:

Cursed be the sinews that could bear woe after woe
and sorrow hand in hand with brother sorrows! It
were best if they were crushed, as with the force
of falling mountains; then it would be the end of all—
no more to bear . . . But I must be doomed to further
woes, since I can endure so much. [*After a pause, slowly*:]
He said he knew it all, but did not tell me his love:
Not even his eyes; nor did his voice betray
the guarded secret. Instead, led me astray
with his false words, made my prophetic fears
an old wife's logic.
Surely he's banded with my father . . . [*after a pause*]
No, that heartless tyrant, that executioner—
Forgive me, Jesus! O how did these unholy words
rise to my lips, and from what profane recess?!
Did he not bring me here? Yet what does it offer
save salt tears and sighs? Better if these eyes
did not know blessed light, nor these ears
delighted in the lark's sweet song,

Act II

   nor in the drowsy murmur of gliding streams . . .

UBERTO:

   For the love of Our Lord torment me no more,
   Dearest Love! I bore unshared the pain
   of knowledge rather than to grieve you twice
   by causing you to grieve.
   [BEATRICE *breaks into nervous sobbing.* UBERTO *falls down
   on his knee beside her and takes her hand*]
   My Dearest, . . . please! . . . You obscure your sunny eyes
   with these wintry clouds. *She still weeps*
   Torrents of tears do not wash away a fixed sorrow:
   they only submerge it. Let's therefore reserve
   them till having tried to pluck it, we fail (if by
   ill-fate we fail). But now a greater quest lies
   before us: to free us from the iron mesh that Fate
   has warily entangled us in.
   [BEATRICE *has stopped weeping*]

BEATRICE:

   No ray of hope do I see breaking the darkness
   of despair—the snare is strongly woven;
   and what, alas, can startled deer contrive
   to overcome the hunter's wariness?

UBERTO:

   No! Like an enraged lion we shall
   force our way out of the pit.

BEATRICE:

   Time flies with breathless haste! I would
   the sun may never forsake our darkened earth
   but linger about and keep perpetual day,
   that the morning of my wedding may never dawn!

UBERTO:

   Don't say these words, beloved: you shall obey
   your father's will, and will marry—but to none but me—

Valentio Di'Buondelmonte

Not in Florence but in some happier town
where we can freely draw the lighter air of love.
Your look tells me you did not fathom
my meaning yet. We shall steal from this
cursed hell guided by the midnight moon
that shall also be sole witness to our nuptials.
Only steal from this home while all
are steeped in sleep's dulling potion,
and you shall find me waiting.
Now, farewell. [*turns to go*]

BEATRICE:

O stay! I'm sick and faint lest we shall meet
no more! Give me strength, inspire me
with your stern purpose, that I may be able
to fulfill our resolve.

UBERTO:

Staying longer makes parting more difficult.
We must feast our eyes on one another
until tomorrow; but then we shall feast them
for evermore. Besides, I leave my heart
with you, your eternal friend, that shall
support yours with love's great might. [UBERTO *exits*]

BEATRICE:

What strange events have sped before my wondering eyes
in just one day's brief span, beyond the ken of wildest
fancy's flight! I must calmly think them over . . . [BEATRICE
exits]
[*Enter* ODDO, ALDRUDA, *and* LIVIA]

ODDO [*looking around him*]:

I think we're not welcome here. But listen!
What do you say to my proposal?

Act II

ALDRUDA:
>My dull brain has only formed a faint image of your words,
>being slow to comprehend because of advanced age.

ODDO:
>Surely you're well informed about Beatrice's shameful wed-
>ding since it's common knowledge by now;
>so I need not tax your ears by repeating it
>but only repeating what else I've said:
>that though all efforts I generously lavished
>to avert the sacrifice of a guiltless maiden
>on the altar of a selfish person's insolence
>have failed, I'm still steadfastly bent on my intent,
>still would spare the powerless Lamb.
>from the wolf's hungry teeth;
>and having thought of you as most fit to execute it,
>knowing the fertility of their cunning, I've
>hurried to you, as one most fit for its execution;
>to lend me a hand. The fierce vulture masked by
>a dove's soft feathers will soon alight in this calm
>nest to win his easy prey with feigned accents.
>It behooves you therefore (if my request finds
>some favor in your heart, to spread the snare
>that no outlet's left to flee therefrom.
>But your daughter's eyes [*gazing at* LIVIA] can, I think,
>well entangle him in the foils of love. [*hands her a fat purse:*]
>This will better illuminate my meaning to you.

ALDRUDA:
>What, a fee?!

ODDO:
>A symbol of my great esteem for you.
>But why duel in studied accents, since we know
>how to foil each other's thrusts?

ALDRUDA [*taking the purse from him. With cold dignity*]: Thanks.

Valentio Di'Buondelmonte

ODDO:

I must leave you now, with hope of quick success.

ALDRUDA:

Yes, and abide with it until success crowns it with reality.
[ODDO *exits*]
[*aside*] He speaks so well as to convince all those
who don't know him, of what he says.
But what do I care? Haven't I my own ambition too?
Such a bridegroom does not fall on one's way
every day And it's I who have to hunt
for bridegrooms for her! [*nodding towards her daughter*]
While she, like an old recluse, has firmly locked
the gates of her soul and has not left even a window
through which light may pass into that dark
and silent abode, or to communicate
with our earthly life. Does she not, I wonder,
not shiver in the cold night-dew when gazing
the long, still hours onto her soul's starless firmament,
and not fear creep through every channel
and highway to her lonely heart when the bleak
silent winds rage on its desolate plains?
Are there brooks and seas?—they must be
silent, to march her own, I think. [*Aloud to* LIVIA:]
Get behind that door and stay there [*Points to a door at the back of the stage, in the middle*] until I open it to you. [LIVIA *obeys*]
[*Enter* VALENTIO]

VALENTIO:

Good evening, madam.

ALDRUDA:

No greetings for him who accepts a bride through fear.

VALENTIO:

Surely you don't mean me, though

Act II

your words, I think, are otherwise meant.
But if I was so addressed, I would reply
that no man who's a true knight
would accept such a dishonorable bargain.

ALDRUDA:

Then in what way have you accepted Beatrice?
You cannot deny that it was through fear
of the Duke's wrath or else the Di'Amediei's swords!
Leave her who you would marry; choose
this damsel in her place, and be henceforth
a brave and honored gentleman.

VALENTIO:

Believe me, madam, you haven't been rightly informed.
besides, . . . [ADRUDA *stops him with her hand and throws open the chamber door, exposing* LIVIA]
What heavenly vision is this!
Were it not day I would have thought it a dream,
a phantom, a mere shadow! But I think, I think
my eyes have fallen on this celestial form—or
in my dreams, prefiguring it. Or before I put on
this mortal garb. Yes, I've seen these eyes,
these two bright orbs that like twin stars
have since shone in my heart. [*to* LIVIA] Speak,
fair Vision, if you are acquainted
with our earthly speech? But no, I do repent
of my words; for thus you're truer an angel.
Your silence is far more eloquent than all
the arts of Orators.

LIVIA [*to her mother*]:

I marvel at these words' meaning.

ALDRUDA:

Ask your heart: if it has nothing to say
Then, only, will I speak. [LIVIA *blushes*]

Valentio Di'Buondelmonte

VALENTIO [*to* ALDRUDA]:
>Alas! It's now too late.

ALDRUDA:
>No! You can yet have her: don't you dare take
>that step and let the consequences rest on me?

VALENTIO:
>I do dare. [*Steps forward and raises* LIVIA'*s hand to his lips*
>*Enter* LAMB.]
>[*Aside: startled*] O my God!

LAMB.:
>Welcome, most welcome! [*to* ALDRUDA, *pointing towards*
>LIVIA:]
>My friend lives yet in her noble features [*to* LIVIA]
>give me your hand; it makes me feel the warmth
>of youth. [*turning to Valenio*] The maid told me
>Beatrice is ill and so you will not see each other now.
>I know too well this will not please you
>but perhaps it is consoling that this delayed joy
>will be doubly repaid when you will meet. [*to all*]
>Dinner is ready; allow me to conduct you to it.

VALENTIO:
>Do not waste your leisure on me. I will follow soon,
>but first I have to ease myself of some thoughts
>that claim immediate attention. [*All except* VALENTIO *exit.*
>VALENTIO *paces the stage for some time with apparent
>agitation;
>the changes in his expression indicating that a struggle is going
>on within him. Suddenly he bursts ou*t:]
>My God, my God! . . . What? Crying to God
>with the same lips that before long I did forswear!
>O mockery of mockeries! And will God heed my cry?
>No, no; my lips still savor of forswearing.
>Then to whom shall I cry?—to the howling

Act II

winds? My cry, outstripping their unbounded passion,
will make them grow silent with fear . . .
To the reposing mountains?
Like a spasm over the whole wide earth,
my cry will startle them and they will shiver.
To the heaving billows? What use when greater
waves of warring powers break on the shattered
rocks of this poor heart? [*Places his hand on his heart*]
No, rather, this vile heart that did violate hospitality
in its own sanctuary. I will forswear my forswearing.
What! Add one more forswearing? No, No,
the second pledge is null. It was no more
mine to give. Besides, Florence's welfare
rests on it, and shall I prove unworthy
of my friends' trust, in reality a perjurer?
I must uproot this love that has so strangely
Planted in my heart's frailest part,
before its fragile roots grow firm, and extend
in its soft soil and fill it. But alas!
Is it not exceedingly cruel?
No, the crown and masterpiece of cruelty?
To break a guileless maiden's heart? To break hers,
breaks mine. But what evil have I committed
to deserve this? To be compelled to strangle
my first, young love when it's only newly born?
A carefree, honorable man I was when I yielded
to her like a weakling child. But why censure
my frail heart for loving? What heart
can the resistless battering of love withstand?
No No, not when its darts come from such eyes!—
they would make Love itself lovesick!
Is it her fault, then? No!
Could she prevent her eyes from conquering?
And is not love made for youth?—
that lyre whose flowing numbers played
by angelic fingers it is. . . . Then shall I buy
the wisdom of old age, by being false to youth?

Valentio Di'Buondelmonte

No, I will none of it. I'd rather be a lover and a fool
than a sage and loveless. Rather a loving enemy
than a loveless friend. And none shall dare call me
afraid of the D'Amedei. . . .
Then why all this faltering, all these vain words?
If they want war, I am their man. Love will
lead me to victory. In what does Honor lie?—
in serving Love. In what does Power, Truth,
Right, Kingdom consist?—in obeying the call of love.
I did forswear to a Duke? Let the Duke,
If he wishes, demand his pledge of him! *Exits*

ACT III

Scene: Front of Lambertuccio's Castle
Time: Night

[*Enter* UBERTO]

UBERTO:
>How still is this serenest night!
>Now the whole wide world
>is intoxicated with the sparkling wine
>of gilded sleep. Even the nocturnal bat
>reposes while I like some portion
>of night's very self, steal
>in the dark, out-waking all except
>the ever-sleepless host of the skies.
>[*Gazes at* BEATRICE's *window, which looks down on the street*]
>Her room is wrapped in darkness. I fear
>she too has drunk the wine of Lethe—
>eager to wake her to my presence
>but for my fear to wake up foreign eyes.
>Patience, my heart . . . soon will she come
>and then, O bright and gentle moon . . . [*Lifts his eyes to the sky*]
>No: he's pale and wan! Are you jealous
>that I am a happy lover, while you,
>loveless, wander in your vast trackless

Valentio Di'Buondelmonte

    void amidst the alien stars that have
no common bond with you?
For shame, deny the charge, say it's not true;
you, friend to bards and plaintive lovers,
lending ever-heeding ears to their complaints
and sighs, and grow pale and faint with sympathy.
Then lo! You grow envious when they taste
the joys of love repaid with equal passion!
It grieves me O moon to see you grieve
that I am glad. I pray you, gentle moon,
brighten your brow so sullen, that your light
may guide my feet in the path of bliss. [*Enter* BEATRICE]

BEATRICE:

    Your Love! But soft, who have we here? [*Walks towards him*]

UBERTO [*Stepping forward*]:

    And yours! [*They embrace*]

BEATRICE

    Your lips are cold, cold as the winds of winter
breaking through the frozen air. Have the stars
distilled on their crimson petals their cold night dew?

UBERTO:

    The cold is nothing while hearts are warm. Fear only
when they are chilled with love dead. But no more now:
we must away. Look! The betraying streaks of day
from the Orient gates of heaven are rending
the velvet folds of friendly night. Such is our
present lot, beloved: the night of care is giving way
to radiant morning. The sun of love will shine on us
and keep our hearts aflame, and will not set
until our mortal day is over.

BEATRICE:

    No, Love. Pray that it may remain a torch
beyond the gates of death. Let us pray,

ACT III

and let greedy oblivion devour the past. [UBERTO *and* BEATRICE *flee. Enter* PILGRIM]

PILGRIM:

The diligent sun hath begun to rise from his fleecy bed of clouds to start afresh his daily course; but this day he will not plod alone, with worn-out feet his ever-trodden way in the deserted heavens. I shall be his fellow-traveler though our goals be different: his, the western abode beyond the distant mountains, mine, Rome. But only God knows full how many times he will traverse the skies ere I behold myself without the gates of Rome. Rome! Queen of the Capitals of the world and mother to all Christendom, the treasure-casket of the hallowed bones of the antique saints who lived and died there and sanctified the very stones on which they trod and the air they breathed. I shall walk where the Great Caesars once walked, amidst the huge marble pillars and statues carved by dexterous hands, that remain eternal and eloquent, though silent witnesses of the splendor that once was. I will pray for forgiveness in blessed Peter's Church and also in the Church of St. Lorenzo, my patron saint. I will fall on my knees before the Holy Father and kiss his holy feet and he will bless me; and when the day of Our Lord's rising be o'er, I'll betake me back cleansed of all sins, a righteous man of God.
[*Enter* BEATRICE's *maid from the castle, going in the opposite direction*]
Good morrow, Lady.

MAID:

Good-morrow, Sir

PILGRIM:

Why, roses do not open their folded petals till the sunbeams kiss them. By our Lady, you'll make the sun ashamed to rise, seeing that you're prettier than she.

Valentio Di'Buondelmonte

MAID:

Are your words, sir, true interpreters of your thoughts?

PILGRIM:

God forbid that they should be otherwise. My grey hairs and my vocation witness to their truth: *Fructus sciet arboris.*

MAID:

Thank you Sir. But in what language did you last speak?

PILGRIM:

The tongue of the Apostles, saints and friars. [*aside*] Doubtless Christ too spoke it.

MAID:

You should be one of them you mentioned, to speak it.

PILGRIM:

I'm but a poor pilgrim.

MAID:

You are very humble, Sir.

PILGRIM [*gazing at the house*]:

Who dwells within these grim battlements and mighty walls?

MAID:

The lion is known from his den; why, the great and noble Lambertuccio D'Ameidei, my Lord. But I almost forgot: my Lady, his daughter, will wed today; we have preparations to make. I fear I have to leave you, sir. [*Looks towards the castle's entrance as though in fear*]

PILGRIM:

D'Ameidei! Why, that's a happiness not bestowed on everyone; and a wedding too! That's still greater. [*aside*] I wish my journey

ACT III

was not today, then I would have attended it! [*aloud*] My greetings to your Lady and my wishes to you for an early wedding.

MAID:

Sir, you're very kind!

PILGRIM:

Kindness is a quality of God Himself; but let me not delay you longer. Good day.

MAID:

Good day, good pilgrim, and remember me in your prayers.
[PILGRIM *exits*]
[*Enter* TOMASSO *as the maid is going in the opposite direction*]

MAID [*smiling*]:

Good morning, master Tomasso!

TOMASSO:

Good morning. Why this unusual greeting?

MAID [*scolding*]:

Why, master Tomasso! Your words surprise me. Don't I greet you every morning with the best courtesy in the world, in no way worse than gentle-bred ladies?

TOMASSO:

I don't deny it. But you're false to your nature in being gay.

MAID [*annoyed*]:

Better than be false to a wedding-day! [*Turns to go*]

TOMASSO:

There, there! Do not take my works to heart. If I wanted to have you dislike the wedding, I myself would have disliked it; but I'm glad with all my heart about it.

Valentio Di'Buondelmonte

MAID [*slyly*]:
>O, you're becoming...

TOMASSO: [*eagerly*]
>For God's sake, out with it! My very breath hangs on it.

MAID:
>As gentlewomen say: "impertinent"!
>[*Embarrassed,* TOMASSO *is at a loss for an answer*
>*The* MAID *laughs at his embarrassment. The voice of*
>LAMB.'s *voice, from the castle, is heard*]
>Tomasso, Tomasso!
>[LAMB. *is seen standing on the threshold of the door*]

LAMB. *[TO Tomasso]*:
>Come, man! This isn't the time for old-wives' tales.
>We've much to do, and the bridegroom will soon arrive.

TOMASSO:
>Yes, Sir. [LAMB. *and* TOMASSO *go into the house*]

MAID [*shrugs and follows them*]

>*Enter* LUCIO, SCHIATTI, *and* RINIERI

LUCIO [*enthusiastically*]:
>How full of warm delights are wedding-days,
>when Nature seems dressed in her best attire
>like a bride adorned for her wedding;
>as though She wants to share and multiply
>a thousand-fold the joys of her young daughters'
>nuptials! Look at the sky, cloudless and bright
>like a child's laughing eyes; and lo,
>the whole wide world seems intoxicated
>with her own sweet beauty.

SCHIATTI:
>Weddings have no joys for me except for the nectar

ACT III

distilled from the juicy golden grape and stored
in ancient casks in the earth's dark womb,
to quench our earthly thirst, and so to drown
our souls in its purple ocean; that they may
ever remain drenched with its warm,
intoxicating dew, dreaming of lovely lasses
with star-like eyes and lips more sweet
than honey-dew, that these soft Naiads,
with light-dusted wings, sip.

LUCIO [*to* SCHIATTI]:

You should have been born in juicy Bacchus' revels
to dote so much on wine!

RIVIERI:

And give the lasses too, a season of their own?

LUCIO:

Yes, the youthful Spring, the bridal-time of year.
For then, roses blow and violets shy; lilies pure
as a virgin's soul; and daffodils, wild Nature's
wan darlings, pale stars of the fields.

SCHIATTI:

Was I born in generous autumn or in the merry
month of May to have a thirst for women and wine?
Youth, even life itself, is an endless thirst
that may not be quenched, like love that
no satiety of sipping nectar from Love's flower knows.
The poet has a thirst for loveliness in cloud and flower,
wave and viewless thought;
and therein lies his delight. The sage
has a thirst for wisdom and seeks
to quench it. Some have thirst for yellow gold:
an insane thirst sometimes, and pursue this selfsame end
with minds and hearts attuned to it.
All men have their own: let me have mine! Lucio

Valentio Di'Buondelmonte

> But if this thirst may not be quenched,
> what use to toil and sweat for it in vain?
> Better that we strive to kill it in its frail infancy
> than to cause us fever and suffering when it grows up.

SCIATTI:

> By my faith, these are true words . . . [*Enter* LAMB.]

LAMB.:

> Welcome friends! You honor me as rarely
> as the rain visits the thirsty desert!
> How do you fare, Lucio? And you, Rinieri?
> How about you, friend Schiatti? Do you still
> dote on wine?

LUCIO [*smiles*]:

> Schiatti, like a true and constant lover,
> never forgets his love. He made it known to us,
> before long, how anxious he was to have her company.

LAMB.:

> She's good, if she does not becomes one's master,
> and thereby urge him to what does not become a man.
> But this day she shall be our host, to entertain
> our light, merry fancies with generous joys,
> make us shun the use of sober reason,
> and by our deeds belie our true selves. [*Enter* ODDO]

ODDO:

> What does this gathering mean? Has anything
> unnatural befallen you? [*Pretending to remember*]
> Yes, the wedding! Forgive my memory that holds
> its mirror imperfectly before my mind. [*Talks to himself*]
> Surely *he* would prefer a bride for fetters or exile,
> or to wed by threats and frowns!—
> a madman's wildest fancy would not be
> as strange a thing as that!

ACT III

LAMB.:
>Your words remind me you still harbor
>a darkness in your heart. I almost forgot it.
>But remember: soon I'll enthrone him in my heart
>like a second love, beside the first, his present betrothed
>and his future-wife. Or like a newborn son
>not of the flesh but of the soul; for what becomes
>one with Beatrice becomes one with me.
>Remember this also: he will become a brother to you.

ODDO [*sarcastically*]:
>No, a nephew!

RINIERI [*trying to change the subject*]:
>We're like soul-forsaken boys without the bride!
>Pray, how fares she?

LUCIO:
>Soon she'll rise from those sweet dreams
>to sweeter reality; and then would rather
>keep awake forever.

LAMB.:
>Sublime reality! When dressed in her white gown
>(a lily enfolded in her lily-laves),
>perhaps the Angels will descend from Heaven
>to join the ceremony, mistaking her for one of their throng!
>[*The* MAID *passes. To the* MAID:]
>Wake up your lady: she has overslept herself,
>[*Re-enter* MAID *after a while, crying*]

MAID:
>Ah me! The Lady! O woe is me! The Lady!

LAMB.:
>What does your wailing thus way mean?!

Valentio Di'Buondelmonte

MAID:
Oh, the Lady, the Lady Beatrice is gone! Woe, woe! She's gone!

ODDO:
She seems to have lost her wits by some strange sorrow. [*To the* MAID:]
How now, woman? Explain!

MAID:
She's not in her bed—the bed is cold—she's nowhere. O the Lady!

SCHIATTI:
Enough!
[*All rush into the house,* then *all reenter with* TOMASSO]

LAMB.:
Beatrice, Beatrice! Cruel, cruel name! It makes
my lips bleed when they breathe it.
No more Beatrice to greet my heart with her
sweet voice. She's fled like a brief, brief dream—
Oh does a dream return? More cruel question!
The only star that burnt in the night
of my lonely soul is no more. . . . Cursed Fate,
that have made my unwilling eyes
witness my daughter, yes, my very flesh and blood
leave me in the autumn of my life
to face alone the frosty winds of winter
and descend unlamented into the eternal grave.
Why has death not visited me before this
has come to pass, that I might have surrendered
myself to His embrace, and pressed his frozen lips to mine?
Then would I have been spared this torture—torture
worse than death. For is not a hope-deserted man
a walking-death, a ruined castle, through whose
prostrate pillars no breeze of hope blows.
The very incarnation of Misery!

ACT III

O that she had been a mother; then surely
she would not have forsaken me. [*A tear rolls down his cheek*]
Unmanly intruder! You would not have dared to swell
in these proud eyes that made a many stout-hearted soul
tremble but that I bear within my breast a father's
womanly heart. Ah me! That such a gentle maid as you
should wound my heart more sorely than the sharpest
swords of foes. . . .

SCHIATTI:

Compose yourself. What use to linger and lament
our mishaps rather than seek to remedy them?
Lame grief only chills the willing hand of action.

LAMB.:

You have not been a father, friend . . .

ODDO [*to* SCHIATTI]:

You speak right. We must act. [*to* TOMASSO] Get ready
the swiftest horses in the stable and prepare yourself
for a human chase. [TOMASSO *starts to go*]
Stay a little. . . . [*Turning to the others*]
Why do you silently look in one another's face,
as if seeking council? Will no one offer
his powers to seek Beatrice? Remember
she must have stolen away with a Lover.
She may be desperate.
Let him who wants to go look for to sword.

LUCIO & Schiatti [*together*]:

We are your men.

ODDO:

Well then, decide among yourselves who will go
to Pisa, who to Rome, and who to Venice. Ride
your horses and bear in mind not to return without Beatrice.
[*Exit* TOMASSO, LUCIO, *and* SCIATTI *hurriedly*]

Valentio Di'Buondelmonte

RINIERI [*musing on what happened*]:
>Great God, how she deserted him! Why? Was she
>in love? Did she not love her father? What, love
>wars with love? Most horrible war! All this
>in the gentle bosom of Beatrice, silently,
>with no outward mark?
>Lightning should have convulsed the face of the heavens;
>thunder, his herald borne on the wings of the swift
>winds, should have proclaimed the civil strife
>in the four corners of the world; while the vast
>seas should have swelled and roared with indignation.
>But the war is done, too soon alas! And now, behold
>the vanquished father, yoked with tears and embittered
>memories. Cruel Fate, that Man should reap the thorns
>of sorrow for sown love. [*Enter* LORENZO, FRANCESCO, *and* BERNARDO]

LORENZO:
>No longer tax your patience to keep alive
>the dying beams of expectation in your eyes.
>If I guess right the bridegroom will be
>with us soon—we see him enter the Di' Donati house.

FRANCESCO:
>Yes, not long ago, while we were on our way here.

BERNARDO:
>His feet scarce seemed to touch the earth; as if
>by nimble spirits borne; or that he feared
>lest he tread too hard upon his Mother Earth
>and by great joy to cause Her pain.

FRANCESCO:
>His every movement seemed in sweet accord
>with inward harmony. Even the living air
>he seemed to fill with the fragrance of joy.

ACT III

BERNARDO:

>One could grow happy in his happiness, to see his
>brimful eyes reflect the fire glowing in his heart
>deepening the crimson hue of his cheeks.
>He was, indeed, a very poet in rapturous frenzy.

FRANCESCO:

>I suppose he did not see us for oblivious joy.

ODDO [*aside*]:

>Brava Aldruda! My confidence was not misplaced.
>The darling robin has been entangled
>in your daughter's enticing beams
>easier than I dared forecast. But rest assured,
>he shall not long remain in your possession.
>*Aloud, pretending indifference*:
>I fear you have to summon all your powers of patience,
>contrary to what Lorenzo would have it.

FRANCESCO [*to* ODDO]:

>Why? Do you suspect a fraud?

RINIERI:

>There's nothing to suspect. He must have gone there
>to accompany Lady Aldruda here.

ODDO [*sarcastically*]:

>Why not Livia?

LORENZO:

>Why do we dally in barren arguments? Soon
>we shall know the truth. If he means to keep his pledge,
>he must be shortly here.

BERNARDO [*to* LAMB.]:

>What hour was fixed for the wedding?

Valentio Di'Buondelmonte

RINIERI:
>That hour was left behind some time ago. Yet
>It's useless now to speak of perjury (if perhaps he
>forswears his pledge), after the mishap that befell us.

ODDO:
>Away with your painted logic! Pour it in coward ears
>to match their listening fear, not into the ears
>of those of the D'Amidei sprung.

LAMB. [*to* ODDO]:
>The charge is yet unproved. Try not in vain
>to seduce me to the use of arms.
>He's been till this very day an honorable gentleman.

ODDO:
>Your eyes must be dim not to see the dazzling truth!
>Unlawful eyes see in thralldom his inconstant heart.
>If you falter still I must suppose that sorrow
>stole your manliness!

BERNARDO:
>By God! Then he shall curse the day he was born!

LORENZO:
>He'll have a hard time from us, I swear!

FRANCESCO:
>Death to the perjurer!
>[*They talk excitedly, simultaneously, so that only a confused mixture of oaths and threats is heard*]

LAMB.:
>Peace, peace my friends. Let us talk more calmly.
>[*The others, not listening to him, together*]
>Death to the perjurer! [*resigned*]
>Be it as you will. [*very coldly*]
>Bring me my sword.

ACT III

ODDO:
>You need not trouble with this affair,
>leave it to me: my sword is eager to meet his.

LAMB. [*Suddenly in a sad voice*]:
>You shall fight only a human foe, while I must fight
>far more dangerous foes: foes that make one start
>from gentle sleep to molten fires that scorch his flesh!
>Foes not outside but within. Myself against
>myself divided. Myself my enemy and my heart
>the battlefield. [*Recovering his calmness*]
>You shall fight him man to man, sword to sword,
>so you shall have no foul play, but honorable combat.
>Now I must retire to myself: to dark silence,
>to seek some repose. [*Exits*]

ODDO [*aside*]:
>My brother pays too slavish homage to empty rules. What!
>My life endanger again, and face the Devil's sword?
>No foul play! Ha! Ha! He shall have a dozen daggers
>stick to his soft hide, the churl!

RINIERI:
>I've no more here. [*Exits*]

ODDO [*to* LORENZO]:
>Do you know a dagger's use?

LORENZO:
>And more!

ODDO [*to* BERNARDO]:
>And you?

BERNARDO:
>And a mace too. Francesco and I.

Valentio Di'Buondelmonte

ODDO:
> Well then, I need your skill. Let us proceed and I'll unfold my mind to you. [*They exit*]

Act IV

Scene: Ponte Vecchio, Florence
Time: Easter Morning, 1215

The conspirators, concealed within the courts and towers of the Ameidei

Enter two citizens dressed in holiday clothes

1st citizen: I wish our good Lord had risen oftener. It had done us a great good, who find scarce an hour to draw lightly the free air and stretch our aching sinews in easeful rest.

2nd citizen: Aye, brother; but for these holidays when we forget out daily work we would become simply mechanical, forget all day long of fire and hammers and bellows, or awls and leather and old shoes, of high prices and low earnings. What is worse, these accursed thoughts chase us even in our dreams, as though to mind us even then of our eternal trades.

1st citizen: Whilst in holidays one passes a pleasant day with his friends and family, conversing and jesting on idle matters leisurely, fondling the while one's children; and in the afternoon, after a warm dinner of meats and soup stroll lazily without the city-gates amidst the scenes of Nature till the sun sinks low, or betake oneself to a tavern to empty a few cups of good old sack.

2ND CITIZEN: But poor devils, we are compelled by fear of starvation to sweat even on God's day, as though He made that day only for those knights who loiter about the streets the livelong day, to cure their boredom by brawls and thrusts, or drowsy in noisy banquets and endless revelry in all manner of excessive drink and heavy foods like swine, blissfully ignorant of the thorns of life. [*Enter* 3RD CITIZEN]

3RD CITIZEN: Good morrow, brethren.

1ST *and* 2nd citizens [*together*]: Good morrow, brother.

3RD CITIZEN: Will you not to church this morn?

1ST CITIZEN: Yea, by and by.

2ND CITIZEN: The day is young yet. *Enter conspirators at back of stage*

1ST CITIZEN: These look not like holiday-makers. They seem bent on unholy deeds.

2ND CITIZEN: They rejoice in the Lord's rising with instruments of war, methinks!

3RD CITIZEN: God protect us from the wiles of the devil!

1ST *and* 2nd citizens [*together*]: Amen! [*Distant sound of church-bells is heard*]

[*Together*] Christ hath risen from the dead!

3RD CITIZEN: Come, brethren, let us away; the bells call us to holy mass. [*Exeunt* CITIZENS]

[*Conspirators come to front part of stage conversing in low tones*]

Act IV

Oddo [*says something to* Bernardo *in a low voice.* Bernardo *shakes his head knowingly*]

Bernardo:
>Beatrice. . . . It reminds me of her flight.
>Who would have thought that she could be returned so quickly!

Francesco:
>Fair chance smiled on them when they met the pilgrim
>outside the city-gates—was it not he who spoke to them
>and made them know it was to Rome these lovers aimed?
>He must have keen eyes to notice them in the early morning.

Oddo:
>Pilgrims have keener eyes than their vocation demands,
>it seems to me.

Lorenzo:
>No matter. Had they parted company before
>They'd seen the pilgrim, the knowledge gained
>might well not served them. One might not have been
>the equal of such a desperate lover.

Francesco:
>True.

Oddo:
>But I deem it unwise of them, when once they
>had compelled him to yield his most unlawful prize,
>to have him spared. They should have eased him
>of his freedom. For I've misgivings that he will be
>fool enough to cherish in his heart the thought
>of high success through a second attempt,
>when he failed once. Now that the fault is done,
>and may not be undone, we must keep strict watch
>to foil such an attempt.

Valentio Di'Buondelmonte

LORENZO [*impatiently*]:
>Let the dead past flatter itself with what attention
>we rendered it: the present is our interest. [*to* ODDO]
>Do you have any strong assurance that may ease
>the doubts in my skeptical heart? It tells me that
>Valentio will not pass this way today:
>you know the heart is prophet.

FRANCESCO:
>Then will you have us heed such an uncertain guide,
>and with an old dame's credulity, let
>this day pass; this morning that we've awaited
>with a miser's strict account, to attend again
>on another occasion to execute our intent?

ODDO [*to* LORENZO]:
>There is no greater liar or knave than the heart.
>It's ever there to lead our wandering steps astray
>making us our own poor fools; ourselves
>our laughing-stocks; at once the actors and
>the audience. What makes Valentio go
>to his swift doom if not his heart?
>I believe he'd rather lose life itself
>than not see his Love this Easter morning.
>I know these lovers well. My friend;
>don't trust, like them, your heart.

BERNARDO:
>What if he does suspect an ambush? He cannot be
>as thoughtless as not to know that we will not
>slavishly accept his outrageous perjury.

ODDO:
>You credit him with more forethought than you need. Bah!
>Who allow their hearts to be conquered
>by the frail charm of feminine art
>cannot be too careful. No, not Valentio!

Act IV

Let us therefore be in readiness that when
he comes he may be as quickly dispatched.
[*Utters a short dry laugh*]
Be quick to action when you see him.
Don't tarry until he handles his sword,
or else he will cause us a Hell of trouble.
Yes, by himself, with the four of us.
By the Devil! He's no mean wielder of the sword. [*aside*] Were
they my lips that uttered "dispatched quickly"? . . .
And yet, is not the heart that would have
the brief moments of his moral agony expand
and so extend so as to fill the whole expanse of time to its
utmost Poles?
No, more; that in these sweetest moments,
Time, that light hare-foot runner, may pause
in His endless track to gather breath;
so might my joy be proportionate.
But here's the worst portion of all.
For I must be content with his death, which may
(who knows) be the very best of goods!?
For might not death, which we all dread,
be but the path to greater joys denied
to the living?—What irony, what playful irony
in Fate's most solemn act!
[*Enter* VALENTIO, *gaily "attired in a vest of fine woolen cloth, a white Mantle thrown across his shoulders and the wedding garland on his Head." As soon as he reaches the "time-worn" statue of the Roman god Mars, which dominates the plaza, the conspirators attack him*]

VALENTIO [*trying to snatch out his sword*]:
Ha! Trying your skill on Easter Morning?!
[*With his mace* SCHIATTI *fells him to the ground, and at the base of this grim Idol the daggers of* ODDO *and his furious kinsmen finish the savage deed*]
O you cowards!

Valentio Di'Buondelmonte

[*Dies—with the bridal wreath "dangling from his brow a bloody and Ill-omened sacrifice"*]

ODDO [*aside*]:

Rejoice, my soul, and O my eyes, drink deep of vengeance's richest beams! Drink till satiety bid you to pause—not less; for truly such sweetness makes gall the nectar the gods on High Olympus sip; and makes Love (that fools deem sweet), blush with crimson shame! Such is this joy that simpletons can never know! [*aloud*]
Go, enjoy yourselves for this occasion!
Revel! Be generous with wine!
I've drunk *my* part! [*points to the corpse*] [*They exit*]

[*Enter* LIVIA *and* STEFANO. *They are unaware of the body*]

STEFANO:

Why does my Lady tax her tender body
by walking such a distance?
If you will allow, I'll proceed alone,
and quickly bring you the news.

LIVIA:

If love bids me go to the frozen Pole I would obey!

STEFANO:

Be it as you wish, my Lady; though I still think,
since you've waited much before this day,
your patience may endure a little more.

LIVIA:

Not so, Stefano: my heart can keep no more within
its bounds the love that has welled up with great
travail as of childbirth, since I saw him last. This
pain is augmented if it's not bestowed on him. [STEFANO *looks around him, and accidentally sees the body. He turns pale and is unable to reply.* LIVIA *notices that something was wrong*]
Why do you gaze at me with such distracted eyes?

Act IV

STEFANO [*with difficulty*]:

> It's nothing worthy of your attention.
> Just a pain that sometimes visits me
> and then as suddenly goes away.
> But I beseech you, my Lady,
> to heed my past words.

LIVIA:

> No, you shall go home. You seem to be sick. I'll go alone. [*She
> starts to continue her way and catches sight
> of* VALENTIO's *body. She utters a stifled cry and is
> about to faint.* STEFANO *supports her. Pathetically:*]
> Tell me it's not true ... that my Love still lives ... Oh, speak!
> ... [STEFANO *remains silent. Then in a parched voice:*]

STEFANO:

> Let us flee from this fiendish place! [*Tries to make her move*]

LIVIA:

> Oh no, divide me not from him! [*Falls on the body. Faintly:*]
> Speak to me, my Love. Speak. I've come, your Love, Your
> Livia. ... would you stay silent in this way forever ... ?
> [*Her tears fall silently, mingling with his blood.*]
> [*She places her hand on his forehead*]
> Ah me! Death's frosty dew has chilled your blanched brow. ...
> [*Sees the deep gashes from which blood continues to well*]
> Your precious life is ebbing with your precious blood, and
> mine too is ebbing with it. ... Will no one stop these dark
> gashes, yawning abysses that have reached to your heart,
> through which Death unveils Himself, from pouring blood
> and more blood?!
> Ah me! That this, your heart, the sacred shrine of Love,
> should thus be subject to sacrilege,
> and be trampled underfoot ... !
> [*Enter* UBERTO, *deep in thought*]

Valentio Di'Buondelmonte

UBERTO:

Fool! Unhappy fool! To let these feelings chill
My resistance by the force of number, nothing more!
They should have forced my breath away before forcing
my heart to yield his Love! What cruel mercy, not to relieve
me of my life; as though death were not sufficient punishment
for love! But they did not know that I was already bereft
of more than life, and so could die no more. They've left
this shadow to roam beneath these imprisoning battlements,
as though its sphere, not as of your rapturous thrill like
the quiver of the leaves in the soft wind, or like the heaving
of the lyre under the frenzied fingers of the bard, but with
a mad tempest of woe and with a heavy heart, made heavier
by the remembrance of lost happiness, bitter for sweetness
flown; with painful consolation that in this dungeon of the
body a heart is still free to love.
[*He lifts his yes and sees* VALENTIO's *body, but does not recognize it because* LIVIA *hangs on it like a drooping lily. Exclaims:*]
Ha! What do my eyes behold: a graveyard,
a battlefield, a Day of Doom?! Is this God's swift courier bent
over the mortal clod to lift the ever- enduring soul to His empyrean throne? [*Approaches, recognizes* VALENTIO's *body*]
Eyes start from your orbs! Let mine revolting hair stand on
end; and you, furious heart, batter my breast over this foul
earth. Alas, my friend Valentio, drowned in your own priceless blood: you, who often bathed in the moon's golden beams!
For you the boughs shall no more dance in glee,
the nested bird repeat your cherished song,
and thrill at his own sweet voice; and the
morning breeze steal a kiss from your wanton hair, wrapped
with wonder and delight to linger there, forgetful of the theft.
The Harvester's blind Scythe has felled your tender buds while
yet half- opened to life's new-awakened Sun, and left, alas,
the thorns, rude thorns, and harsh briers. . . .
[S*ees the wedding garland that lay stained with blood and the wedding ring*]

Act IV

Ah me, you have indeed been wedded to Death,
the cold-eyed Maid; and this [*pointing to the garland*],
truly your wedding wreathe! Why fallen in eternal sleep?
What heart would smile to see you fallen? [*slowly:*]
He was to wed to Beatrice; where was she then,
Yes, where was she? . . . [*Suddenly he bursts out:*]
A scapegoat, made to bear the wrath of Di'Amedei
for her flight. It would indeed rejoice Oddo—
Yes, killed before the Castle! Why did I not warn him to
beware an anger perhaps creeping in the Night? But it needs
divining eyes to see that woe
would thus be born of bliss. Besides,
could I unveil to him my secret purpose?
What's the use? For he was bold and fearless
as the forest lion, and would have laughed that Death has
fixed his unerring shaft to murder him—
His boldness was his undoing. [*Observing* LIVIA *weeping in silence. To her:*]
Who are you, woman, disturbing him in his repose?
You do not mourn a knight by wetting his cold corpse with
tears, but by bathing him in his murderer's blood!
If he is dear to you, let the fountain of your tears
dry in your bosom by the fierce flame of hate
and the fire of firm resolve to avenge his outrageous death
flash in your eyes! No tears, but crimson blood freely flowing;
and by this grim idol of fire and fury. . . .
[*Pointing to the statue of Mars*]
He shall have it! [*bends over the body*]
Sleep in peace! This firm arm you rescued from the chill of
death shall become to you a second arm
to fell your enemies.
[*Beckons to* STEFANO. *They carry the body away while* LIVIA, *is still bent over her Husband's body pallid features.*]
[*Re-enter simultaneously from opposite sides:* UBERTO, *sword in hand, and conspirators*]

Valentio Di'Buondelmonte

UBERTO:
I had not thought that villains don't dare cross the damned site that witnessed their dark unholy deeds, where every stone is a keen eye, and every pebble a mouth to betray the murderer. You should bury your faces in dark corners, far from human paths lest swift justice overtake you while your hideous face is dyed with blood, and read your crimes written in bloody syllables in your fearful eyes.

ODDO:
Zounds! You pine to join your friend in Hell
that you dare cross my way!

UBERTO:
You speak of fighting?

ODDO:
Beware, rash youth; go if you pity yourself
and break your sword. Or else, by all the fiends of hell you shall soon die a mad dog's death!

UBERTO:
I'd rather break my sword on your back if you weren't worthy only of being beaten with a cudgel!
Come, quick (if you are the one who struck him down) and face my sword.

BERNARDO:
I can no more listen to this lunatic's babble: I'll silence him.

ODDO:
No, wait; let him relieve his mind before he dies. It will serve as a confession.

UBERTO:
No, confess *your* sins first; for you shall die
before these cowards stab me from behind!
Take heed! [*Attacks him. They fight.* ODDO *is wounded*]

ODDO:
 The knave! He's killing me!
 [*The others attack* UBERTO *and overcome his stout resistance, mortally wounding him*]

UBERTO [*dying*]:
 Valentio.... Forgive me, Beatrice... [*Dies*]
 [*The conspirators leave, supporting* ODDO]

Act V

Scene: A room Lambertuccio's Castle

[*Enter* BEATRICE, *talking to herself*]

BEATRICE:
>How changed my God, how changed, and in such
>a brief span! Scarce seems himself, grown old in days
>when others grow old in years. Deeply are traced
>by sorrow's rude finger the lines of pain upon his brow,
>and dark mist hangs in his spark-less eyes.
>The smile still hovers over his convulsed lips, perhaps
>unknowing of his plight, or as painted mask to put off
>curious eyes from secret scrutiny, and so unveil tyrant
>despair in his heart's core, enthroned there
>with ball and scepter, unrivaled lord of his precious
>domain. Yes, growing rich on poverty, fattened on famine.
>How difficult, my God, how difficult to be compelled
>to play the jester's fun or the merry actor's farce
>before the blind, contented audience, while the real
>veiled self behind the stage is hourly stabbed
>with viewless knives in his unattended Tragedy,
>with every jest the actor makes;
>and when the alien others depart, and the actor
>quits the stage, empties his flowing woe on his
>un-consoling pillow, and shakes the solid walls
>with signs and groans: being two selves and seem but one;

Valentio Di'Buondelmonte

himself be not himself: alien unto it.
For I have felt full sorry, my father,
since that most sweet day and bitterest;
when, as ever in your every look and word
you offer your love, you expect to receive no more;
a lonely, hopeless love: love in despair;
a somber light; a shadowed rightness; night in day.
And this, alas, is woe's sharpest pang:
if like a swift meteor this love,
with its own flame itself consumed, or else
if you did but expel it from your heart's Eden,
as came to pass with our First Parents; then
it would have been far easier: it would have caused
me less pain. But is not love perfect in itself,
in itself sufficient, with itself content,
a universe of its own?--What, deceive myself
with these smooth words? But why?
For I love him—who dares say I love him not!
I love him since I learnt what love is;
when clad in naked majesty, revealed Himself,
as God, to Moses, in Sinai.
It's strange indeed to grieve that I have loved:
could I love Him not knowing love? Does love
bid us love and yet not love? Embrace Him
by drawing away from his extended arms?
To love without loving?
Love envies Love? Is it not one, undivided?—
Oh, were that all! I have learnt the loss of love:
Uberto, greatest of my woes; theme of my bitterest tears—
it's not that you are dead; for Love is life
and death is not where life is.
There is no love and death. Death is powerless
to divide what love has joined; and I could fly so easily
the dark dungeon of life if death were the only
prison-gate between us; but you has forsaken me
by your very death. It's plain that dire failure
has dragged love's radiant star, that scattered

Act V

its joy-laden beams, outshining the Evening Star,
like a falling meteor, down the abyss of despair
and quenched it there; thus purposeless in life's
myriad ways, no more a pilgrim to love's
distant shrine, you staked your precious life
for a low gain: prodigal in your most precious
possession, disposing it as though it were your own alone,
not also mine. No, mine far more. Revenge?
What mockery!—love a beggar at friendship's door,
entreating to be heard in vain; no, driven off like a dog
by proud oblivion!—a paramour into whose
credulous ears is poured the dew of endearments sweet,
yet soon to be forgotten when on another maiden
displays her more gaudy charms,
dexterously arrayed, before the raptured eye! What
truth reviled; order made chaos, reality unreal, subject
made Lord and Lord with menials placed?!
For lo! Love, lord of the soul, before whose sovereignty
friendship should bend the knee of meek homage,
has risen in rash rebellion, his throne usurping,
claiming obedience low of him who knows how
to receive, but not to give. Indeed, avenge a friend!?
I must never harbor in my breast the hope of death:
death serves me not; it is a night that has a morning—
love's death is an eternal sleep, unbroken
even by the dream of happiness past;
a death without resurrection. To wake from death wakes
me not from death—I must turn my face towards warm life.
By very life I shall forsake him as he has forsaken me
[*starts as from sleep*] live! Did I say "Live"?
Live, when life's sap is dried? I love him yet!
Infernal powers, I love him yet! Love is invincible!
[*Pulls out a dagger hidden in her bosom. To the dagger:*]
Let you cold steel destroy what love has built—let
nothing remain to tell that love had once dwelt there ... [*Stabs herself in the breast*]
Oh ... [*Dies*]

Valentio Di'Buondelmonte

[*Enter* Livia]

Livia [*with an expressionless face, goes slowly towards the body*]
I had not thought death so simple, so sure
in its embrace, so swift in its cure!
But one brief moment, and all is over. . . .
[*Bends over* Beatrice's *body and pulls the dagger dripping with blood from her breast; gazes at the dagger for a few moments, then brings it to her breast. Frightened:*]
No! I dare not! [*Throws the dagger down, shuddering*]
The path of death is lonely and dark,
with what horrid dangers perhaps beset?
What hideous monsters, what abysses gaping wide
that make the blood to freeze and to obstruct
its channels to the heart no mortal thought may fathom,
no fancy paint. Ah me, to sail alone on that wide
and dark sea, a creature frail as I, with no beacon
or pilot-star to steer my course to the farther shore.
Prayer and faith have no use to me;
rather they'll be a warning and a threat,
eternal curse, God's preordained just sentence
to those rebellious spirits that with proud insolence
and most impious hands reject and stain
God's vested garment—Hell, where love
and peace do not dwell but writhing pain and wailing, midst
the most abhorred of men; and there
how shall I stand before God's throne to claim my Love?
Alas, if Hell itself could unite us I'd do it. [*Pauses*]
Then since the Gates of Death are barred for me, I'll
to a convent, where the iron bars and the sacred garb
doubly imprisoning my ancient self, will make me free like
one newly born from the womb, to build
a newer life upon the ruins of the old. There will I
fast and pray, and all the sacred rites observe,
to bring God's balm to bruised souls,
though none to me, like a sage well read
in Galen's art who can't administer to his own ailments.

Act V

For I know full well how vain it is to flee
from a living self (though fettered), that will haunt
my prayers and loneliness, and silent nights,
and all my old life will rise as from the tomb
with all life's pulse, and then, fleeing
will there be none. Oh, forgive me Love;
fleeing from my sweetest memories, from life
in death shall become the bond between
my love and me, until the day of union dawns. Ah,
when it dawns.... [*Her eyes are filled with tears*]
[*From outside the sound of swords and steel mixed with shouts are heard*]
Hack! Burn! Death to Donatei! Death to the Buondelmonti!
To the Castle! Hang the old hag! Hang the old witch!
Livia Oh God!
[*Casts one last look at* BEATRICE's *body, then exits hurriedly*]

www.ingramcontent.com/pod-product-compliance
Lightning Source LLC
Chambersburg PA
CBHW071439160426
43195CB00013B/1968